POLITICAL AND SCIENTIFIC ARTICLES

VOLUME 2, SECOND EDITION

GERALD MCISAAC

Printed in the United States of America

ISBN 978-1-959483-70-0 (sc)
ISBN 978-1-959483-69-4 (hc)
ISBN 978-1-959483-68-7 (e)

Library of Congress Control Number: 2023938617

History
2024.06.05

TABLE OF CONTENTS

1   Impeachment of Trump and Trial by Senate 1
2   Students Protesting Climate Change 10
3   War With Iran 17
4   Prepare to Storm the White House! 27
5   An Appeal to Scientists 35
6   The Trial of Donald Trump 41
7   Abolish the Electoral College 48
8   Appeal To Professional People 54
9   Appeal to Women 65
10 Form an American Independent Citizens Society ... 72
11 The Crisis Intensifies 77
12 Bloomberg and the Democratic Primaries 84
13 Sanders As Front Runner 92
14 Unions Against Sanders 99
15 Primaries and Caucuses 105
16 South Carolina and Super Tuesday 111
17 Sanders and the Electoral College 118
18 Sanders, Super Tuesday and the Corona Virus 124
19 Super Tuesday and the Electoral College 130
20 March 10 Primaries, Super Tuesday 2 138
21 Left: Study Marxism, Join the 2 Parties! 146
22 Too Small To Succeed 155
23 Depression and the Federal Reserve 165

24 Economic Stimulus Package- Ha! 177
25 Ichthyosaur In Okanagan Lake? 185
26 Corona Virus and Statistics................................. 190
27 Corona Virus and the Surge................................. 198
28 To the -Former- Small Business Owners.............. 203
29 America Edging Closer to Dissolving 211
30 Medical System Close to Collapse........................ 217
31 Revolution In Industrialized Countries 223
32 Now What To Do? 228
33 Platform of an American Communist Party.......... 238
34 Separate American Republics Forming................. 246
35 Mosasaurs, Plesiosaurs, Ichthyosaurs et. al. 253
36 Depression: A Crisis of Abundance 257
37 An Appeal to Working People.............................. 262
38 Towards a World Socialist Republic 271
39 Three Trends in the Revolutionary Movement...... 281
40 Merger of Black and Working Class Movements .. 289
41 Create More Autonomous Zones!.......................... 297

1

IMPEACHMENT OF TRUMP AND TRIAL BY SENATE

The holiday season has brought news of great joy to countless people. President Donald John Trump is now officially impeached. Millions of people could not have asked for a finer Christmas present. It is just too bad that such a gift cannot be wrapped and placed under the tree.

The cheers and celebration of the progressive people on the Left stands in stark contrast to the weeping and wailing of the reactionaries on the Right. The day the House of Representatives passed two articles of impeachment is a day which will "live in infamy". They are afraid this is the beginning of the end of the American Empire. We can only hope and pray they are correct.

The House of Representatives, or the Congress, is currently controlled by the Democratic Party, led by the Speaker of the House, Nancy Pelosi. The Democratic Party presents themselves as the party of the middle class, the "little guy". By contrast, the Republican Party is presented as the party of the rich, the business people, those who are responsible for creating wealth and jobs. This great wealth of the capitalists is supposed to "trickle down" to the "less fortunate".

This fairy tale is a world of fantasy which the capitalists, the bourgeoisie, have created. In their dream world, there is no working class, the proletariat, just as there is no capitalist class, the bourgeoisie. The only class they refer to is the middle class, and that includes almost everyone. It may help to think of this as a Sesame Street for adults.

This imaginary creation of the capitalists stands in stark contrast to reality. The fact is that we live under capitalism in its highest form, that of monopoly, technically referred to as imperialism. Those who support monopoly capitalism, imperialism, are of course referred to as imperialists. These people are completely reactionary. There is absolutely nothing progressive about imperialism. The imperialists, and those who support the imperialists, are concerned only with the maintenance of the wealth and power of the class they represent, the monopoly capitalists, the bourgeoisie. That is the point which has to be driven home to the vast majority of working people, the proletariat.

The two mainstream political parties, Democrats and Republicans, serve the same class. The party bosses, those who are card carrying members of the parties, are those who work "behind the scenes", and "call the shots", or "pull the strings" of their "puppets", those who are elected to political office. Excuse the metaphors, but the use of such popular terms may be the best way to persuade the vast majority of working people, the proletariat, of the existence of classes, of the antagonism between the classes, and the absolute necessity of becoming politically active.

As Speaker of the House, Nancy Pelosi has long resisted the calls from the progressive members of her party, the Democrats, to impeach Trump. No doubt the Democratic party bosses decided not to impeach Trump, as they decided that is not in the best interests of the class they serve, the bourgeoisie. Yet the pressure "from below", which is to say the members of the public, the working class, proletariat, and the middle class, technically referred to as the petty bourgeois, was so intense, she was forced to take action. Hence, two articles of impeachment.

So far so good, all in accordance with the law of the land, the Constitution, which states quite clearly that it is up to the House of Representatives to impeach a president who is suspected of being guilty of "Treason, Bribery or Other High Crimes and Misdemeanors". Now it is up to the Speaker of the House to send those articles of impeachment to the Senate, so that Trump can go on trial and be judged by that Senate. All of this is in accordance with the Constitution.

It is not by accident that Nancy Pelosi was dressed in black at the time of the passing of the articles of impeachment against Trump. Such attire is traditionally worn at funerals, as an indication of mourning. She also scolded the members of the Democratic party who started to applaud, much as a school teacher corrects a class of students who are misbehaving. Shame on you, members of The Squad!

Now Nancy Pelosi is looking for a loop hole, some way to prevent or at least delay such a trial. She is quite cheerfully pointing out that the Constitution makes it clear that the articles of impeachment must be referred to the Senate, but it does not say when those articles must be sent. This tactic of stalling is characteristic of the bourgeoisie. Perhaps they think the working class will lose interest and forget about such little details as removing Trump from office.

The journalists are reporting that this stalling on the part of Pelosi provides her with "leverage". Perhaps a reality check on the part of the journalists is in order. Even the Senate majority leader, a fellow Republican of Trump, is wondering just what "leverage" there is in *not* forcing him to *not* conduct a trial, *one to which he is dead set opposed!* He is being threatened with *not* having to deal with the articles of impeachment, which is the very thing he so desperately wants!

No doubt Pelosi will present the articles of impeachment to the Senate at the point when the pressure "from below", from the members of the public, the working class and the middle class, becomes sufficiently intense. As the working people are so focused on this impeachment process, that should take place any day now.

The details of the trial have yet to be worked out, and that is a bone of contention. The Democratic senators want a proper trial, complete with witnesses and documents. The Republican senators want a "kangaroo court", a quick vote to acquit Trump of all charges, ignoring all evidence to the contrary. Such a procedural detail requires a simple majority vote, and as there are fifty three Republicans but only forty seven Democrats, it will require four Republican senators to "cross the floor" and vote with the Democrats, in order to have a proper trial.

By contrast, two thirds of the Senators have to vote guilty in order to have Trump removed from office. In effect, the

Senate is the jury, but not to be confused with an impartial jury, as is required in a court of law. The majority leader of the Senate made it quite clear that he will vote to acquit, regardless of the evidence presented, and will pressure the members of his party to also vote to acquit. We can expect nothing better from such people.

This is not to say that the anticipated trial by the Senate does not concern us. Far from it. Our goal, the goal of Marxists, conscious people, Communists, is to raise the level of awareness of the working class, the proletariat. We want them to become aware of themselves as a class, with interests which are diametrically opposed to the interests of the capitalists, the bourgeoisie. The best way to do this is to use examples of that which concerns them, and that certainly includes the anticipated trial by the Senate. We must make it clear that Trump is not the problem. Whether he remains in office or not, the class he represents, the bourgeoisie, will remain in power. Nothing of substance will change.

With that in mind, we can also suggest that all American citizens, members of the public, working people as well as middle class, take that one extra small step of joining the two political parties, Democrat and Republican. After all, the capitalists say that if we do not like the way things are, then we should "change it from within". The least we can do is take them at their word. What better way of changing the system from within than by becoming card carrying members of both parties? As party bosses, American citizens can flood Washington with Leftist people. Just think, Leftist people running for office on behalf of both parties. This should keep campaign expenses down to a minimum, as such people will be running against themselves. Who cares if they go to Washington as a Democrat or as a Republican? For that matter, both parties can endorse someone such as Sanders for president. As for those who are concerned with the age and health of Sanders, bear in mind that other Leftist people are available. Such people include Michael Moore. I think that lad would make a fine candidate for president.

Incidentally, I am not joking. I have the utmost respect for that gentleman. He is clearly a self made man, a member of the working class who has become successful as a result of great sacrifice and hard work. He truly cares about working people.

Of course, the choice of a person to run for president is a little detail for Americans to decide.

Most members of the public, including the most advanced members of the working class, are confused concerning the events unfolding in Washington. Most reasonable people would assume that the members of the White House Resistance, those who published an editorial in the New York Times, would welcome the impeachment and removal of Trump from office. After all, they announced their intention to stop Trump "one way or another". What better way to stop Trump than by impeachment and removal from office?

Yet those same people have decided against that course of action. Much as they would love to remove Trump from office, they are even more afraid of the revolutionary motion which is sweeping the country. They are well aware that almost all Americans are watching this impeachment process. Their greatest fear is that those same Americans will in turn become politically active. In short, the bourgeoisie are afraid of revolution.

The situation is certainly revolutionary. Many millions of Americans, those who were formerly apathetic, are now becoming politically active. They are taking an interest in the impeachment process and the anticipated trial by the senate. It is safe to say that the vast majority of these people are honest, hard working, law abiding, tax paying citizens. It is also safe to say that the vast majority of politicians who represent these people are anything but honest, hard working, law abiding, tax paying citizens. Now it is a matter of persuading these honest working people that they are members of a working class, with interests which are diametrically opposed to the interests of the capitalist class, the bourgeoisie. Most politicians serve the class of capitalists, and that class is determined to hold onto power, at all costs.

The anticipated trial by the senate of President Trump should help to raise the level of awareness of the working class. At the very least, it gives conscious people, Marxists, the opportunity to explain that which is taking place. The fundamental principles of Marxist revolutionary theory have to be explained. We can use this as an example of bourgeois democracy, which is nothing more than democracy for the bourgeoisie. At the same time we can compare this to proletarian democracy, in the form of the Dictatorship of the Proletariat, which is a far superior form of democracy.

The fact is that many millions of people have been closely watching the impeachment proceedings. The reason they are so interested is that they are deeply dissatisfied, not content to live in the old way, demanding change. They are instinctively gravitating towards socialism, as yet unaware of that which they are experiencing. By contrast, the capitalist, the bourgeoisie, are supremely well aware of that which is happening. They know that they cannot live and rule in the old way, must now change their method of rule, but are unsure how to proceed. This is the very definition of a revolutionary situation.

It is just a matter of time before the crisis matures to the point of explosion. The working class could spontaneously revolt at any time. It could happen any day now, or the capitalists could force the issue, perhaps with a declaration of martial law. Either way, the revolution can best be understood as a force of nature, an act of God, because that is exactly the case. It is not about to hold off until the working class, the proletariat, is prepared to seize political power. It is absolutely essential now to prepare people for the revolution and the subsequent Dictatorship of the Proletariat. Workers now must be trained for the duties they will have to assume after the revolution. What better way to train them for leadership roles than by becoming card carrying members of the two parties, party bosses?

No doubt there are a great many people, including those who consider themselves to be Marxists, who are of the opinion that the capitalists, the bourgeoisie, can be overthrown by the "democratic process", that of voting into power Leftist people. Such is not about to happen, and the best way to persuade the millions of working class people of this fact is to encourage them to do just that. It will no doubt be interesting to see the response of the bourgeoisie to this challenge to their authority.

The point we want to drive home – not only to the working class but also to the optimistic middle class intellectuals – is that it does not matter how many Leftist people we send to Washington. Our goal is to raise the level of awareness of the working class. With that in mind, our goal and our slogans should read:

Prepare for the Dictatorship of the Proletariat!

2

STUDENTS PROTESTING CLIMATE CHANGE

Lately a young lady, a lovely 16 year old by the name of Greta Thunberg, has been making headlines. She was recently voted the Time Magazine Person of the Year, beating out other finalists, including Donald Trump. So of course Trump did that which he does best. He insulted her. Perhaps Trump should be nominated for the Ignoramus Person of the Year. He certainly has my vote.

Greta Thunberg is a student activist, famous for initiating a School Strike For the Climate. This has apparently triggered a student protest movement, one which has since become wide spread. This is excellent news. It is an indication that the revolutionary movements in various countries, being spear headed by America, France and Hong Kong, are spreading to the younger generation, as well as other countries.

The last thing we want to do is to discourage such revolutionary motion, on the part of the students, as well as people who are not so young. This in no way changes the fact that the climate is constantly changing, and has been since the creation of the world.

We may point out that recently, by which I mean within the last hundred thousand years, there have been three ice ages in North America. In terms of geological ages, a hundred thousand years is a very short time, which is the reason I use the word recent.

At the time the glaciers covered the continent, a great deal of water was tied up as ice, so to speak, and the levels of the oceans of the world were considerably reduced. No doubt this had an effect on the climate in various parts of the world, so we can say that the dramatic drop in temperatures on one continent was indirectly responsible for climate change on a global level.

We can honestly say that no one knows precisely the cause of the ice ages in North America, although various theories have been put forward. Nor do we know the causes of the warming of North America, which resulted in the melting of the glaciers. The only thing we know for sure is that people had nothing to do with this. At that time, there were far too few people, and the only green house gasses they released were in the form of camp fires.

It may help to point out that classes exist all around the world, and that it is the class of capitalists, the bourgeoisie, who are the problem. Their one and only concern is that of making a profit, and not just any profit, but the maximum possible profit. If this huge profit results in the fouling of the water we drink and the air we breath, then so be it. They consider this the cost of doing business.

To say that the climate is changing as a result of the burning of fossil fuels is at best a stretch. Further, to say that the science supports this belief is supremely optimistic, as the scientists are careful to say that which the capitalists want them to say. To say anything else is to commit career suicide, as our political leaders, the politicians, are in the service of the capitalists, the bourgeoisie.

I realize that is a strong statement, and I am sure that a great many people will be insulted by this. Yet I stand by that which I have said. I have been conducting research for many years, challenging theories in various fields of science. As a result of that research, I have written several books documenting the distortions and outright lies of the scientists, some of whom are highly respected. At the same time, I have provided directions for determining the existence of a great many species, all of which are thought to have gone extinct a very long time ago. They are not extinct. They can be located quite easily and inexpensively. The scientists have not discovered them because the scientists are careful not to look for them.

With the help of the members of the public, common people, we will very soon prove that there was no mass extinction of dinosaurs. That "mass extinction" is a mere fairy tale, as is the "mass extinction of megafauna" here in North America, at the end of the last ice age. Further, there was no mass extinction of reptiles. That includes the flying reptiles, pterosaurs or pterodactyls, and several orders of swimming reptiles, fresh water as well as salt water. We should add that within each reptilian order, there are probably dozens of species. It is safe to say that most reptilian species, if not all, are predators, man eaters. Lest we forget, there is a separate species of human living among us in North America, commonly referred to as Bigfoot or Sasquatch. Naturally, the scientists are careful to ignore all evidence of their existence.

May I suggest that all this talk of "climate change due to greenhouse gas emissions" is a "red herring", a decoy dreamed up by the bourgeoisie, in an effort to divert the revolutionary movement onto some harmless path of social reform. As so many people are now deeply concerned with climate change, it appears to be having some effect.

In the interests of bringing clarity to a situation which has been deliberately obscured by the bourgeoisie, may I suggest to all climate activists, and not just students, that they consider the wars that are currently raging in various parts of the world. These wars are a natural result of the competition between the so called "great powers", the highly developed countries, those who are determined to rule the world. At the same time, consider the poverty and slums, the hunger, the homeless people living on the streets of those same countries. The capitalists, the bourgeoisie, the people in charge of those countries, can afford to spend mountains of money on war, but cannot afford to feed and house their own citizens. Then there are the immigrants, people desperate enough to risk their lives, in an attempt to find a better life for themselves and their children. These people are being thrown into prison, separated from their children, who are also being thrown into prison. Their only crime is that of being poor and desperate.

That is merely a small sampling of the butchery and misery for which the capitalists, the bourgeoisie, are responsible. Bear in mind that those are the same people who control the careers of the scientists. Any scientist who dares to suggest that I am right, is sure to commit career suicide, never again to earn a living working in any field of science. That is just the way it is.

Those are the same people who swear that climate change is taking place as a result of green house gas emissions, and that we have got to change our way of life. Or words to that effect. It is difficult, if not impossible to figure out exactly what they are saying, if only because they are trying to confuse the issue. In that department, that of spreading confusion, they are doing a splendid job. I just do not believe a word they are saying.

I am certainly not suggesting that those who are politically active, opposing climate change, should quit being politically active. Far from it. I am suggesting that those same people consider that which I am saying, and perhaps assist in the search for one or more of the animals which I have listed in my books. The directions for finding those animals are clear and simple. I can also suggest that Americans, in particular, should become card carrying members of the two mainstream political parties. That way, as party bosses, they can send Leftist people to Washington, and those politicians can fight to oppose climate change.

Incidentally, I consider the search for these prehistoric animals to be a part of the class struggle, merely a different battle ground. If nothing else, they are part of our heritage, one of which we have been robbed. Aside from that, there is a desperate urgency involved in locating the flying reptiles, pterodactyls, as they are currently preying upon women and children. Females of child bearing age they attack because they smell the blood, and children are easier to pick up and carry away. This takes place in the darkness in open areas, the victims are taken to caves in the mountains, and the remains are never recovered. In the vast majority of cases, the families of these women and children never know what happened to their loved ones. Their suffering, mental anguish, never ends. I can only express my most sincere condolences, and regret that I do not have better news.

It is also true that these same animals are able to kill horses and cattle, the livelihood of so many farmers. Their livestock is found dead and mutilated in the morning. As long as their livestock is left outside after sundown, this death and mutilation will continue. Sad but true.

I have also given direction to prove the existence of the Sasquatch, or Giants, as I refer to them. Those who first make contact with these people, a separate species of human, will no doubt be supremely proud. That is the dream of every scientist.

The energy and enthusiasm of those involved in opposing climate change will soon be focused on the revolutionary motion, that of overthrowing the bourgeoisie and establishing the Dictatorship of the Proletariat. At the moment, there are various protest movements in the country, fighting for social reform, of one sort or another. It is only when those same movements come together to fight for scientific socialism, that real lasting change will take place. Until then, the best those well meaning members of such protest groups can hope to achieve is paltry reform.

The correct Marxist understanding of the class struggle has to be made available to all people, working class and middle class, young and old, students and retirees. All must be encouraged to become politically active. The revolution is on the horizon. The only way forward is scientific socialism. The only alternative is a utopian dream. The bourgeoisie have to be overthrown and crushed under the heel of the working class, the Dictatorship of the Proletariat. Only then can we develop clean sources of energy, clean up our environment, providing one and all with clean water and clean air. This will only happen when humanity is relieved of the profit motive.

In the interests of uniting the various movements towards the common goal of overthrowing the bourgeoisie, of raising the level of awareness of all working people, we can suggest the following slogans:

Scientific Socialism!
Dictatorship of the Proletariat!

3

WAR WITH IRAN

The day January 2, 2020, is a day which will "live in infamy", as far as Iran is concerned. It is the day the United States assassinated a top Iranian general, as well as nine other Iranian citizens. It is the day the United States provoked a war with Iran. Just as surely as the Japanese attack on Pearl Harbour was an act of war, so too the American killing of several top Iranian officials is an act of war. The question is not a matter of "if" the Iranians will retaliate, but "when" the Iranians will retaliate.

The Iranians have already announced that they plan to resume their production of nuclear weapons. They have also announced their plan to attack several American military targets. In response to this, Trump has announced that if that happens, the American military will strike fifty two Iranian targets, cultural as well as military. It should be noted that any attack on civilian targets is considered to be a war crime.

Now, more than ever, it is imperative for conscious people, Marxists, those who are aware of the existence of classes, to bring to the working class the awareness of themselves as a class. This act of aggression, if not outright war, is characteristic of the imperialists. Explain to working people that imperialism is monopoly capitalism, and that such people, the imperialists, the super rich, the billionaires, the bourgeoisie, are completely reactionary. They will go to any length to preserve their wealth and power. This act of war against Iran is merely one example. The fact that countless people could end up dead is of no consequence, at least as far as the imperialists are concerned.

Trump has justified this act of mass murder, the killing of ten Iranian citizens, as a defence against an "imminent threat" on the part of General Seleimani. Of course, Trump was careful not to go into any details. Perhaps Trump expects us to trust him, to take him at his word. Just how stupid does he think we are?

It is to the credit of the journalists that they have documented thousands of instances of Trump lying, and that in the mere three years that he has been president. The man lies constantly, for any reason and for no reason. Clearly the man is simply not capable of being honest. If I was the charitable sort – which I am not – I would say that the man is sick, in desperate need of professional help. But I maintain that Trump is not sick. He is merely a typical member of the class of monopoly capitalists, those who are technically referred to as the bourgeoisie, and all such people are bare faced liars. Trump is not a sick man. Trump is a lying man. Trump is a typical bourgeois.

There is a reason Trump "allegedly" ordered the murder of those Iranian men. I use the word "allegedly" out of respect for all courts of law. The fact of the matter is that he brags about ordering them killed, but that has yet to be proven in a court of law.

No doubt there are many readers who cannot imagine Trump being arrested and charged with any crime, much less murder. After all, he is a billionaire, and such people are immune from prosecution. "Money talks", as is the age old expression, and in fact it talks loud and clear. But now working people are also "talking", and if anything, the working people are talking even louder and more clearly, or at least more clearly than ever before. The days of the bourgeoisie getting away with any and all crimes, including murder and sexual assault, are a thing of the past.

As for those who are skeptical -and I welcome such a healthy attitude- may I point out to everyone the fact that recently a number of rich and famous people, including celebrities and billionaires, have been charged and convicted with various crimes. Perhaps the case of Jeffrey Epstein is the most revealing.

Epstein was a convicted sex offender, a pedophile, which is to say a child molester, commonly called a "skinner", who was charged with several very serious crimes. He was locked up awaiting trial when he allegedly committed suicide. At least, that is the official version. The unofficial version is that he was murdered. Either way, there are a great many very rich people, members of the bourgeoisie as well as members of the nobility, who are quite happy to hear that he is dead. One of those members of the nobility is a member of the British royalty, a son of the queen, no less. Numerous other billionaires are suspected to have paid Epstein a great fortune for the honour and privilege of raping underage girls. The death of Epstein may have gotten them "off the hook", but only temporarily. As the revolutionary motion gains strength, other victims, under age girls at the time of their rape, are sure to step forward.

As Trump is the head of state, he is no doubt aware that it is against international law to order the murder of others, whether military people or civilians. It is also against international law to target civilians, in case of war. It is not clear that all members of the American military are aware of this. The fact is that it is not just Trump who could be charged with the murder of those ten Iranian men. The military members who carried out that order can also be charged. The International Criminal Court, the I.C.C. has ruled, many years ago, that "just following orders" is not a legal defence.

It is to be hoped that the pilots who are ordered to bomb civilian targets, as well as the operators of missile launchers who are faced with similar orders, will give this serious consideration. Better to face charges of failing to obey illegal orders, rather than face charges of war crimes at the International Criminal Court. Worse still, such people could be sent to Iran to face charges. That is perhaps the worst night mare of every American military member.

The Iranian delegate to the United Nations, the U.N., has lodged an official complaint, properly so. As a result of this, the U.N. may intervene and request the I.C.C. issue a warrant for the arrest of Trump and all others responsible for the killing of those ten Iranian citizens.

As for those who consider this to be a joking matter, may I suggest all consider the fact that as long as Trump is president, the head of state, he probably cannot be arrested and charged in any court. As soon as he is out of office, "all bets are off", so to speak. Staying in his home country, in this case the United States, will likely prevent him from being arrested. On the other hand, as soon as he sets foot outside the protection of the country, he is likely to be arrested. That of course is assuming the I.C.C. issues a warrant for his arrest.

The same is true for the military personnel who carried out the illegal order and fired the missile that killed those ten men. The only difference is that they can be arrested at any time, if they leave the protection of the country, as they are not elected officials.

This is what we can expect under the current political climate. That could change, and change most dramatically, and much sooner than most people think.

Of course I am referring to the approaching revolution and the subsequent Dictatorship of the Proletariat. At that time, the capitalists, the billionaires, the bourgeoisie, will be separated from their wealth and power. They will be crushed under the iron heel of the working class, the proletariat. We will first and foremost protect our women and children. Sex offenders and child molesters, skinners one and all, will not be tolerated. The same is true of thieves and killers. Trump and the members of the military would do well to bear this in mind. The threat of appearing before the I.C.C. may well be the least of their worries.

The ten Iranian citizens were killed within the borders of Iraq, and the government of Iraq has responded by ordering the expulsion of all American military personnel. No doubt the Iraqis want no part of a war with Iran. As this military presence is little more than an occupying force, it is very likely that this "order" will simply be ignored by Trump.

Immediately before this killing of the Iranians, those same Iranians mounted that which I would refer to as a probing offensive. Within the capital of Iraq, there is located an American embassy, which is considered the most safe and secure of all American embassies. The walls and doors were thought to be safe from all assaults. In addition, there is a secure zone around the embassy, guarded by Iraqi troops, those who were trained and equipped by Americans. This zone is referred to as the "Green Zone", for some reason. This provides the embassy with an added level of security. Or so they thought.

The Iranians decided to determine the security of the embassy, and were no doubt pleasantly surprised. A rather small detachment of men, perhaps a couple hundred, unarmed, were sent to the Green Zone. The Iraqi troops guarding that zone could easily have driven those men away, but they did not. They allowed those Iranians to approach the embassy and attack it, with hand held weapons. Many of the Iraqis, those who were supposed to be guarding the embassy, joined in the assault. The steel doors were broken down and the embassy was penetrated, over a period of two days. The embassy personnel were forced to retreat to a more secure location within the compound. At that point, the Iranian commanders gave the order to pull back. To go any further would have invited American fire by machine guns, artillery and aircraft. As the troops were disciplined, they did as they were ordered.

The American military is claiming they repulsed an attack on their embassy by the Iranians. That is not saying much as those men were not armed. They are careful to ignore the fact that the Iranians broke into the American embassy and determined precisely the weakness of the American position. The American embassy is not at all secure. Further, at the time the war breaks out, they can expect the Iraqi forces, including those whom the Americans have trained and equipped, to join them in fighting those same Americans.

The reason for this impending war with Iran is that Trump has been impeached. He is facing a trial by the Senate, as is required by law, and must be worried. If convicted, he will be removed from office. Most people are of the opinion that is not about to happen, as the Senate is firmly controlled by the Republican Party, the GOP. I am not so sure of that, and apparently Trump is not so sure either. Hence, a war with Iran, as a means of forestalling any trial. Perhaps he is of the opinion that with a good war waging, people will lose interest in removing him from office.

As I write this, the Speaker of the House is still hanging on to the articles of impeachment, "negotiating" with the Republican majority leader of the Senate, concerning the rules of the trial. As the last thing that majority leader wants is a trial, I doubt there is a great deal of negotiations taking place. He is very likely telling her what she can do with those articles of impeachment. That is not something which is mentioned in the press. But then, it is not fit to print.

No doubt there are a great many people, either current or former members of the middle class, who are well aware of this. To such people I can only say, pass it on. The working class has to be made aware of themselves as a class. That requires repetition and the explanation of the technical terms, as it is also necessary that working people be aware of those terms. It is only the working class, the proletariat, that can lead the revolution. The middle class, the petty bourgeois, can and must, bring this class awareness to the proletariat.

The middle class, the petty bourgeois, or at least the remnants of that class, are simply not capable of leading the revolution. They can and will take part in the revolution, assisting the working class, but their duty now is to raise the level of awareness of the proletariat, to prepare the working people for the Dictatorship of the Proletariat.

As for those who complain that the proletariat is not prepared to assume political power, I can only respond that you are right. That is a fact, just as it is a fact that in Russia, 1917, the proletariat was even less prepared to assume political power. The revolution was forced upon them, as Karensky was prepared to surrender Saint Petersburg, the capital of Russia, to the Germans, as a means of crushing the revolution.

The point is that if we wait until the proletariat is prepared to seize political power, completely trained, the revolution will never happen, as the bourgeoisie will make sure that preparation never happens. The best we can do is prepare them for their approaching dictatorship, as it is very likely that the bourgeoisie will soon force the issue.

For that reason, I am encouraging all Americans to become card carrying members of the two mainstream political parties, Democratic and Republican. As such, they will become "party bosses", in positions of leadership. It may help to think of this as training for the Dictatorship of the Proletariat, because that is precisely what it is. Of course it is not reasonable to expect the majority of working class Americans to join the two parties. It is reasonable to expect the most advanced strata of the proletariat to do just that. They in turn will receive valuable training in leadership roles, which will prove to be most valuable after the revolution, when they are placed in positions of authority, crushing the bourgeoisie, under the Dictatorship of the Proletariat.

Bear in mind that the most advanced workers are the leaders, while the less advanced workers pay strict attention to their advice.

In the interests of persuading as many American to join the parties as possible, I suggest the use of slogans. These should appeal to people from different age groups. This is just the beginning, and as people become active, they can also be encouraged to read Marxist literature. The experience they gain in the class struggle will soon persuade them of the correctness of our position.

These slogans are meant as suggestion only. For the younger generation, possibly:

Free Tuition!
Abolish All Student Loans!

For the older generation, the seniors:

**Free Medical!
Increase the Pensions!**

For the unions and all working people:

Increase the Minimum Wage!

For the sports people:

**Defend Our Bill of Rights!
Hand Guns Yes! Hand Grenades No!**

It is to be stressed that no one should be badgered to join the two parties. It must be strictly on a voluntary basis. Under no circumstances should this lead to confrontation. Those who are not familiar with computers, such as the seniors, should be offered assistance. Stress the fact that as party bosses, they get to decide the person to go to all state capitals, as well as to Washington. There is no need to tell them that they should nominate someone who is sure to fight for their interests, as common people are not entirely stupid. On the other hand, Washington is filled with bourgeois boot lickers who naturally assume we are just that. It is high time we showed them the error of their ways.

As usual, in the interests of international solidarity, and for the benefit of those who are more advanced, I can close with my usual favourite slogans:

**Workers of the World, Unite!
Scientific Socialism!
Dictatorship of the Proletariat!**

4

PREPARE TO STORM THE WHITE HOUSE!

President Trump ordered the execution of ten Iranian citizens recently, including a high ranking member of their military. This killing took place on Iraqi soil, without the knowledge or approval of any Iraqi official. The Iraqi Parliament has immediately responded by ordering the removal of all American military personnel from the country.

The American military in turn released a memo, written in the convoluted language which is characteristic of all bureaucrats. As they phrase it, the American military "in due deference to the soverignty of the Republic of Iraq, and as requested by the Iraqi Parliament and the Prime Minister, will be repositioning forces over the course of the coming days and weeks to prepare for onward movement...Coalition forces are required to take certain measures to ensure that the movement out of Iraq is conducted in a safe and efficient manner...We respect your soverign decision to order our departure."

It is strange that the bureaucrats, both civilian and military, take great pride in phrasing simple statements in the most twisted manner they can imagine. Their expression "to prepare for onward movement" is another way of saying that they are going to retreat. Perish forbid that they should use simple language that common people can understand.

According to the press, this memo was signed and delivered by an American general who is serving within the country of Iraq. It is clear that he respects the "soverignty of the Republic of Iraq" and the authority of the "Iraqi Parliament and Prime Minister". As that is the case, it is equally clear that he does not belong in the American military.

The American high command, which is to say the Joint Chiefs of Staff, JCS, most emphatically disagree with that memo. They say that it was a mistake, a "draft", and should never have been released. They have no intention whatsoever of pulling troops out of the "soverign Republic of Iraq", regardless of the wishes of the "Iraqi Parliament and Prime Minister". The American high command, including the JCS, has no respect for the Soverign Republic of Iraq. American troops are occupying that country and they fully intend to continue to occupy that country.

The squabbling does not end there, not by a long shot. It extends to the very top of the American high command, both military and civilian. As president, Trump is the "Commander in Chief of the American Military". As such, Trump has the final word. His final word is that the American military will not only continue to occupy Iraq, but in case of a war with Iran, will target "cultural centres".

This stands in stark contrast to the statement of the Defence Secretary and the Chairman of the Joint Chiefs of Staff. They say they will "follow the law of armed conflict". That is the law which forbids the targeting of civilian or cultural centres. Such actions are considered to be war crimes.

It is safe to assume they are referring to the approaching war with Iran, as the American military already killed ten Iranian citizens. Perhaps they are of the opinion that this act of mass murder does not fall under "the law of armed conflict". They could be right, as such people like to "split legal hair". This in no way changes the fact that ten men are dead. It certainly makes no difference to the members of their families, whether the people responsible for this act of mass murder are charged with an act of terror, or murder, or war crimes, or crimes against humanity. But then the penalty is very likely the same.

This in no way changes the fact that the Secretary of Defence and the Chairman of the JCS have both stated that they will "follow the law of armed conflict", *in direct contradiction to the orders of their Commander in Chief, President Trump.*

The fact that they prefer to abide by the laws of war imply a certain level of intelligence on their part. They simply do not want to be charged with war crimes. It is doubtful that they have taken this stand on any humanitarian grounds, because they are staunch defenders of imperialism, and such people have no humanitarian tendencies. They are merely marginally more intelligent than Trump, which is not saying a great deal.

Assuming Trump orders the destruction of cultural centres, it remains to be seen if the members of the military will carry out that illegal order.

On the home front, so to speak, the situation is equally confused. The members of the House are already considering further articles of impeachment, even though the first two articles of impeachment have yet to be delivered to the Senate. In popular terms, this is considered putting the "cart before the horse".

The Speaker of the House is setting the standard, an example many other members of the House are quick to follow. She has yet to submit the articles of impeachment to the Senate, so that the trial by the Senate is postponed. She is also considering a vote on a "war powers resolution to limit President Trumps military actions regarding Iran...military hostilities with regard to Iran to cease within thirty days".

It is not often that we witness such touching displays of starry eyed optimism from such high ranking members of the American government. Perhaps the Speaker of the House has missed her calling. She really should have joined the Peace Corp.

Perhaps someone should remind her that Trump just ordered the execution of ten men, almost certainly provoking a war with the soverign country of Iran. He fully intends to target cultural centres, as soon as that war begins. He is well aware that these actions are in violation of international law, and he simply does not care. So now the best the Speaker of the House can come up with is to limit him to thirty days of "doing his worst"? What makes her think that Trump will respect such a "war powers resolution"? What planet is she from?

The only surprise is that the White House Resistance, those who published an editorial in the New York Times, have yet to take action. They vowed to stop Trump "one way or another", and yet have failed to do so.

It is clear that the American imperialists are deeply divided. They appear to be well aware that they cannot rule in the old way, and must change their method of rule. They simply cannot agree on the change. The immediate problem is Trump, and they cannot even agree on the best way to remove him from office.

This is class war, soon to break out into open conflict. It is the class of monopoly capitalists, the bourgeoisie, the ruling class, against the working class, the proletariat. Now is the time to strike, as the enemy is deeply divided, squabbling among themselves. It is entirely possible that they have decided that the best thing they can do, is nothing at all. They may have decided to allow Trump to run amok, to provoke a war with Iran, knowing full well that it is a war they cannot possibly win, as any alternative could well provoke a civil war, a revolution.

Even though a war with Iran could -and will- create terrible damage to the country, the American imperialists are prepared to pay that price.

Now the American bourgeoisie consider Trump to be a "loose cannon", which is precisely what he is, and formerly decided to stop him, "one way or the other". The trouble is that they are also well aware of the revolutionary movement which is taking place, and they are afraid that any action they take against Trump could trigger a revolution. There is nothing which scares them more than the threatened loss of their wealth and power, being crushed under the Dictatorship of the Proletariat.

Perhaps we can compare the current situation to that of Russia in 1917. Karensky, as head of the bourgeois Provisional government, was well aware that the situation was revolutionary. His greatest fear was that the peasants and workers, the proletariat, would rise up and overthrow the government of the ruling class, the bourgeoisie. As a result of this, his plan was to surrender the capital, Saint Petersburg, to the Germans. Only the November 7 -new style calendar- revolution was able to prevent him from carrying out this act of treason.

In the current situation, Trump has apparently been given a free hand to go to war with Iran. At least, it is safe to assume that the Iranians will retaliate, if only because they said they will. This will almost certainly lead to a war in the Middle East, and not just with Iran. We can expect several other countries in the region to become involved, not because they love Iran, but because they hate America.

This Middle Eastern War is almost certain to cost countless lives and cause great damage to America. But just as Karensky was prepared to sacrifice the capital of the country, in order to prevent a revolution, so too the American ruling class is prepared to ruin this country. What ever it takes to preserve their wealth and power.

All indications are that the revolution is closer than most people realize. War is on the horizon, and as Marx phrased it, "War is the midwife of revolution". This is not to say that war is necessary to start a revolution, because it is not. It is to say that the First World War gave birth to the Russian revolution. The next war with Iran could give birth to the next American revolution.

As that is the case, and as most middle class intellectuals are familiar with the details of the Russian revolution, it is perhaps appropriate to suggest a slogan for the fortunate few. It may help to serve as a not so subtle hint for them to get active. They are well aware that at the time of the revolution, Karensky was holed up in the Winter Palace of the Czar. He and his fellow government officials were guarded by troops of the Savage Division, if I am not mistaken. The precise details are not as important as the fact that there were a limited number of troops available to protect the members of the Karensky regime. The reason for this is quite simple. Most of the army was at the front, fighting the Axis forces.

The point is that at the time of war, the ruling class is at its weakest, due to the fact that most of the troops are at the front, not available to crush any revolutionary out break. As a result of this, the revolution is more likely to be successful.

The intellectuals to whom I am referring are well aware of this, just as they are aware that at the time of the storming of the Winter Palace, other key sites were also secured. These included communication centres in Saint Petersburg and Moscow, as well as railroad stations, key bridges and sea ports, all across the country. A similar uprising must be carefully planned for the American revolution, but on a much larger scale. There are a great many cities in America, as opposed to the few in Russia in 1917. We can expect the American officials to hole up in the White House, much as the Russian officials holed up in the Winter Palace. So at the time of the uprising, it is necessary to storm the White House, but also numerous other key sites. Capital Hill and the Pentagon, for example.

With that in mind, I can only stress the fact that the uprising must be carefully planned and coordinated. That is where the middle class intellectuals come into play. Feel free to follow in the footsteps of Marx and Lenin, fellow middle class intellectuals. Make plans for the insurrection. Your slogan can be:

Prepare to Storm the White House!

5

AN APPEAL TO SCIENTISTS

As I write this, the trial, by the Senate, of President Trump is just starting. That is certainly a step in the right direction, and long over due. The importance of the trial lies not so much in the outcome, but in the fact that so many working people, including those who were formerly apathetic, are now taking a keen interest in the "democratic" process.

It is also a fact that the ruling class, the bourgeoisie, have arrived at a stage of crisis. They can no longer rule in the old way, and must change their method of rule. As yet, they are floundering, unable to decide precisely the new method of rule. The organization they have established, which I refer to as the White House Resistance, has yet to make a decisive move. This is to say that Trump has yet to be stopped. They are afraid that any move they make on Trump could trigger a full scale revolution. They are also afraid that if they do not stop Trump, he could trigger a full scale revolution.

Either way, revolution is on the horizon, and could break out any day. Now is the time to raise the level of awareness of the revolutionary proletariat, to bring to the proletariat the awareness of itself as a class. The scientists are in a unique position to do this, in that they can document the lies and distortions of the bourgeoisie, as written in the scientific textbooks. Some of these lies are quite flagrant. This may help to drive home the point that the bourgeoisie are a pack of liars and hypocrites.

Here is a short list of the outright lies of the scientific textbooks:

Dinosaurs went extinct 65million years ago, even though birds are dinosaurs.

There are no mass extinctions of reptiles, even though there were 5 mass extinctions of reptiles.

The megafauna in North America survived three ice ages, even though they went extinct because they could not survive climate change.

The dire wolf is extinct, even though it still exists, but only as a remnant population of an extinct species.

The Jefferson ground sloth is named after Thomas Jefferson, who described one such animal, even though it is extinct.

Astronauts could never have survived a trip to the moon, because they would have been exposed to massive doses of radiation, even though astronauts walked on the moon.

Countless reports, by credible eye witnesses, of a giant, naked, hairy, bipedal ape, Sasquatch or Bigfoot, which matches the description of gigantopithecus, are disregarded, as that ape went extinct a hundred thousand years ago.

Even more reports of UFOs are disregarded, as the millions of people who have seen these objects are merely delusional.

This is but a small sample of the lies propagated by the scientific community, on behalf of the bourgeoisie, and after the revolution, these lies will be exposed. Now is the time to get ahead of this, to join the revolutionary forces, and not be crushed under the wave of revolution which is about to sweep North America.

No doubt all scientists are aware that to go public with these facts would risk almost certain career suicide. This is certainly a legitimate concern, as most people have responsibilities, families who are counting on them for support. To such people I can only respond that there is strength in numbers. All members of the trade unions can testify to that. Bear in mind that these unions were forced upon the working class. The capitalists gave the workers no choice. In much the same way, the capitalists are also giving the members of the middle class, the petty bourgeois, including the scientists, no choice other than to band together in a fellowship of some sort.

With that in mind, I can only suggest that scientists follow in the footsteps of the proletariat, and form an International Scientific Association. Such an Association would have real power, able to stand up to the bourgeoisie, to demand and achieve legitimate change. Members of all branches of science should be encouraged to join the Association. Possibly it should be extended to scholars and intellectuals. As the Association takes shape, the members can determine such little details. The broader the Association, the more power it will hold. It should not be limited to one country, but to all countries of the world. Now that we have the internet, we would be fools not to take advantage of it. The capitalist are able to ruin the careers of any particular person, but not a whole Association of people.

Such an Association, or at least members of such an Association, could point out that Marx and Lenin were political scientists. They placed the class struggle on a scientific basis. It is doubtful, and probably not desirable, that the Association would advocate the Dictatorship of the Proletariat, but certain members of the Association could do just that. As scientists tend to be highly respected, their endorsement would carry a great deal of weight. This would certainly help to raise the level of awareness of the working class. As a bonus, such scientists would not be a target of the revolution.

Perhaps that requires a little explanation. All scientists can be said to be members of the middle class, petty bourgeois, or at least aware of the existence of classes. If nothing else, their education and life style force this awareness upon them. By contrast, the rather limited education of working people, and the life style of the working class, does not lead to the awareness of classes. These are merely facts that I am stating.

It is also a fact that the working class sometimes gets into revolutionary motion, as is currently happening. I refer to this as an act of God. This is not to say that the members of the working class know what they are doing, because they do not. This is to say that the working class makes history. The current ruling class, the bourgeoisie, is about to be overthrown and crushed by the working class, under the Dictatorship of the Proletariat. The working class is as yet not aware of this.

At the time of the outbreak of the revolution, by which I mean a full scale uprising, the working people will attack those whom they consider to be the enemy. This includes the bourgeoisie, although they are few in number. It also includes the people who support the bourgeoisie, and they are quite numerous. All scientists, and in fact all members of the middle class, would be well advised to distance themselves from the bourgeoisie. Make it clear to the working class, before the "outbreak of hostilities", the revolution, that you are on the side of the proletariat. The alternative will not be pleasant.

With that in mind, I can only stress to scientists and intellectuals the urgency of forming an Association, if for no other reason than as a safety net. Then, those who choose to become politically active can help to raise the level of awareness of the proletariat. Those who choose to not become politically active run the risk of becoming targets of the revolution.

Either way, the revolution will soon break out. The higher the level of awareness of the working class, the smoother will be the transition to socialism, in the form of the Dictatorship of the Proletariat. It is to the advantage of all scientists to make sure this transition is as smooth as possible.

I will close this article with slogans which I hope will soon become house hold expressions:

Workers of the World, Unite!
Scientists of the World, Unite!
Scientific Socialism!
Dictatorship of the Proletariat!

6

THE TRIAL OF DONALD TRUMP

It is a day of rejoicing for countless Americans. Their dreams have come to pass. Their prayers have been answered. Donald Trump has been impeached. He has been placed on trial by the Senate. Hallelujah! Their cup runneth over! This is indeed a day which will go down in history. They got precisely what they wanted.

The only fly in the ointment is that Donald Trump has been completely vindicated. The Senate has ruled that he has not committed any crime which warrants removal from office. He will continue to be president and break any and all laws, as he sees fit. The only political body with the constitutional power to reign in the president, the Senate, has now officially abdicated that power. Donald Trump has now been granted the power of emperor.

Practically the whole country was watching the proceedings, that of first impeaching the president, as an act of Congress, followed by the farce of a trial by the Senate. It came as no great surprise to the vast majority of working people that the Senate merely acquitted him. Almost all members of the working class are well aware, from their own bitter experience, that the "super rich", as they refer to them, can do almost anything they want.

Perhaps the only people who were surprised and disappointed by the outcome were the members of the middle class, the petty bourgeois.These misguided souls, starry eyed optimists one and all, actually thought that it was possible to "change the system from within". They actually thought that their democratically elected leaders would take their oath seriously. As far as those politicians are concerned, their oath, that of "protecting and defending the constitution", is merely a bit of idle verbiage. Their loyalty lies with the class of people whom are commonly referred to as the super rich, and in fact are the monopoly capitalists, the bourgeoisie. It may help to think of the bourgeoisie as the lords and masters of the politicians, because that is precisely what they are.

It may be objected that the members of the House of Representatives, the Congress, voted to impeach the president, against the wishes of the bourgeoisie. That is certainly true, but only because of the extreme pressure "from below", which is to say as a result of the movement of the members of the public, mainly the working class. A great many members of the middle class were also involved in that movement, or at least those who still maintain the petty bourgeois mentality. The middle class has been all but wiped out, but their mentality extends to the working class.

The "trial" of Trump was closely watched by countless people, if only for its entertainment value. A great many people were openly laughing, amused by the fact that for possibly the first and only time in history, a trial was being conducted *without the testimony of witnesses or the presentation of evidence.*

In essence, the "trial" consisted of nothing more than closing arguments. For hour after boring hour, the attorneys for the "prosecution", the lawyers whom had been sent by the Congress, stated countless times that Trump should be removed from office, because he broke the law. This was followed by an equally boring series of monologues by attorneys for the defence, those who argued that he should be acquitted. In essence, they spent numerous hours stating that which Richard Nixon stated quite clearly many years ago: "When the president of the United States breaks the law, it is not a crime."

Without doubt, Donald Trump most emphatically agrees with that statement. Equally without doubt, the Senate is also in agreement.

This is not to say that the trial was pointless. Precisely the opposite. The trial served as a fine educational tool for the members of the public, especially for the idealistic members of the public, including the optimistic members of the middle class. Many of those well meaning people were of the opinion that the democratic process could be used to remove Trump from office. This is possible, but only in theory.

In fact, the ruling class, the bourgeoisie, has established a state apparatus which carefully protects the members of the bourgeoisie. Trump is a member of that class, and as such, is fully defended.

The day before his acquittal, by the Senate, Trump gave a State of the Union address to both houses of Congress, by which is meant the House of Representatives and the Senate. He first gave a written copy of his speech to the President of the Senate, which is of course the Vice President, Mike Pence, and to the Speaker of the House, Nancy Pelosi. She in turn offered to shake his hand, in a gesture of respect and friendship, which Trump ignored. After he gave his speech, she very publicly tore up that paper copy of his speech.

If nothing else, this serves to drive home the point that the country is deeply divided. This is *not* to say that the Democratic Party serves the "little guy", the working people, while the Republican Party serves the "super rich", the monopoly capitalists. On the contrary, both parties serve the same class, the bourgeoisie. It just means that the ruling class, the bourgeoisie, are deeply divided, unsure just how to continue to rule.

They are afraid that Trump will lead the country to ruin, along with their class. They are determined to stop him, hence the creation of the "resistance", an organization which I refer to as the White House Resistance. They are also afraid that any move they make against Trump could trigger a full scale revolution, while not to make such a move could also trigger a full scale revolution. This is commonly referred to as "being caught between a rock and a hard place".

Either way, it is clear that the revolutionary motion is becoming ever stronger. It is also clear that the revolution is being led by American women, many of whom have been the victims of the worst sort of sexual and physical abuse. It is very likely that their bitterness and hatred is growing.

No doubt these women have been closely following other developments in the news, especially the arrest of a convicted sex offender, Jeffrey Epstein. He was in turn charged with several very serious charges of a sexual nature, which included procuring under age girls for his rich friends. In popular jargon, he was a pimp, selling children to the members of the bourgeoisie. Various names of powerful people have been mentioned, including that of the president, Donald Trump, and the Attorney General. No one was terribly surprised when Epstein was found dead in his prison cell. The official cause of death was determined to be suicide, but this has been disputed by other medical professionals.

It is very likely that the victims of Epstein number in the hundreds, if not the thousands, as he trafficked in young girls for many years. Each and every one of those girls feels cheated, deprived of justice, as their abuser, their pimp, is now dead. But then a great many of their clients, the people to whom Epstein sold those girls, are still alive. The last thing those rich and powerful people want is for this to be made public. In legal jargon, this is considered to be a strong motive for murder.

If nothing else, recent events should drive home the point, at least to class conscious people, that we live under the dictatorship of the bourgeoisie. The one and only alternative to this is the Dictatorship of the Proletariat. The bourgeoisie can and must be overthrown and crushed under the Dictatorship of the Proletariat. This calls for revolution, as the bourgeoisie are completely reactionary, determined to maintain their wealth and power. As long as the bourgeoisie remain in power, the exploitation of the working class will continue. Young girls, children, will continue to be sold to the highest bidder and raped. Those responsible for these terrible crimes will continue to be protected by the authorities.

To the victims of those pedophiles, as well as the victims of countless other predators, I can only suggest that you transform your rage and bitterness into determination. Focus on the class of people responsible for your degradation, and not merely one person. Prepare for the approaching revolution. Study the most essential works of Marx and Lenin. Carry the awareness of classes to the working class. Join the two parties, Democratic and Republican, as card carrying members. As well, encourage your family and friends to also join the two parties. Run for any and all political offices, on behalf of both parties. Organize demonstrations to oppose Trump and other members of the bourgeoisie, at any and all opportunities. Disrupt their social functions. Give them no peace. Carry signs that call for the Dictatorship of the Proletariat. Bear in mind that the more famous the celebrity, the more attentively the members of the public listen to them.

It is best to remember that it is the party bosses who determine the candidate to run for any and all political office. It stands to reason that if enough Americans join the two parties, then both parties can choose to support Sanders for president. If nothing else, that should save a great fortune on campaign expenses.

Of course the bourgeoisie will not allow Washington to be flooded with Leftist people, certainly not Marxists, Communists. They will respond by changing their method of rule, and in the process, become more exposed.

The most important thing now is to prepare for the revolution. The more class conscious the working people are, the more smoothly will be the transformation to the Dictatorship of the Proletariat. For now, our posters and banners should read:

Workers of the World, Unite!
Scientific Socialism!
Dictatorship of the Proletariat1

7

ABOLISH THE ELECTORAL COLLEGE

As the journalists phrase it, "the dust has now settled", in the not so little matter of the impeachment and trial of Donald Trump. He has been acquitted, and will continue to serve as president. The journalists are careful not to say that there is a reasonable chance that he will soon be re-elected and serve another four years. That is a nightmare scenario they cannot bring themselves to face.

Instead, they are seeking solace in speculation that Trump may have learned his lesson. No doubt he has learned his lesson, just not the lesson the journalists have in mind. He is reported to have stated, years ago, words to the effect that he was so popular, he could kill a man in broad daylight on Park Avenue and get away with it. Now he has learned that there is some truth to this. The only elected body in the country which has the authority to keep the president in line, the Senate, has just given Trump a blank check. Now he can do whatever he wants.

This is not to say that the people responsible for his impeachment are taking this lying down. On the contrary, they are already taking action. The House of Representatives, the Congress, is preparing further articles of impeachment. It did not work the first time, and in fact the trial by the Senate was an abject failure, so of course they are determined to try it again and keep trying until it works.

The fact is that such a course of action has not worked in the past and is therefore not about to work in the future. Any medical expert can swear to the fact that the expectation of a different outcome, while doing the same thing, is the very definition of insanity. It is also the definition of the bourgeois mentality.

Of course if Trump is once again impeached, then the Senate will once again find him not guilty. That is a foregone conclusion, one which the bourgeois members of Congress cannot seem to grasp. It is also most emphatically clear that the only reason he is president in the first place is because of the Electoral College. After all, Trump lost the popular vote, *but was still elected!*

America is the only country in the world with an Electoral College. It is a remnant of slavery. It was originally set up to allow slave owners to occupy the White House. Historians are agreed that it was the Electoral College which allowed Thomas Jefferson to become president.

At the time of Jefferson, the number of electoral votes of each state was determined by the population of eligible voters of that particular state, and by *a percentage of slaves within that state.* The more slaves within a state, the more electoral votes. It was to the advantage of the slave owners to own as many slaves as possible. The more slaves they had, the more political power. Accordingly, the slave owners in charge of each slave state made it very difficult for any slave to gain his or her freedom.

The American Congress abolished slavery in 1865, with the Thirteenth Amendment to the Constitution. That was absolutely the correct thing to do, but it did not go far enough. That amendment to the Constitution did not abolish the Electoral College. Now it is time for Americans to follow in the footsteps of their revolutionary forefathers and carry on the work of those courageous individuals. It is time to abolish the Electoral College, to add to the Thirteenth Amendment to the Constitution, to honour their ancestors by finishing the work they started.

There is no point in focusing on removing Trump from office through the impeachment process, if for no other reason than that recent events have proven this to be a lost cause. The only value of the process lies in raising the level of awareness of the working class. To remove Trump from office would merely result in the replacement of someone just like him. The current Vice President, Mike Pence, is living proof of that.

This in no way changes the fact that the American public is very interested in political developments. The American working class is in motion, as well as many current or former members of the middle class, the petty bourgeois. This revolutionary motion is being led by women, many of whom are middle class, including numerous victims of physical and sexual abuse. They deserve our heartfelt gratitude and support.

That being said, the best way to support those people is to make clear our position that no change of face in Washington will change the fact that the bourgeoisie is in charge. Nothing of substance will change until that class is overthrown. That change will only take place when the dictatorship of the bourgeoisie is replaced by the Dictatorship of the Proletariat. There is no middle ground.

With that in mind, the American people can demand that their elected leaders in Washington demand a change to the Constitution, in the interests of establishing a more democratic republic. Such an Amendment to the Constitution requires a vote of two thirds of both houses of Congress, which is to say that both the House of Representatives and the Senate must vote for the change. The other way to secure the Amendment is by having two thirds of the state legislatures call for a constitutional convention. I am suggesting that Americans adopt both approaches.

In this manner, ever more Americans will become involved in the political process, on a state level as well as on a federal level. In is reasonable to expect that only the more advanced workers will assume leadership roles, which is precisely what we want. We can think of this as valuable training for the Dictatorship of the Proletariat, because that is precisely what it is.

After the revolution, a new socialist society will be established. The current state apparatus, which has been set up to protect the bourgeoisie, will be abolished. A new state apparatus will be established to crush the bourgeoisie, in the form of the Dictatorship of the Proletariat. The bourgeoisie must be thoroughly crushed, in any and all walks of life. After the revolution, their resistance will be increased ten fold, as their hatred and fury grow, and they will make every effort to regain their "paradise lost". This happened in Russia and it happened in China. Now it is up to us to make sure it does not happen here in North America. Soon, the North American bourgeoisie will be crushed, but with more enthusiasm. We must avoid the mistakes of previous revolutions.

The key thing now is to prepare for the approaching Dictatorship of the Proletariat. After the revolution, workers with very little training, or even no training whatsoever, will be placed in positions of authority. The more training they receive now, the smoother will be the transition to the Dictatorship of the Proletariat, the fewer mistakes they will make, and the more thoroughly the bourgeoisie will be crushed.

It is perhaps best to think of a revolution as a force of nature, an Act of God, because that is precisely what it is. As such, it is not about to wait for people to become prepared. It will happen when it happens, and it is clear that the revolutionary motion is becoming ever more intense. The country is a powder keg, prepared to explode. There is no telling what spark will ignite it. This is all the more reason for conscious people, Marxists, to become more active, to raise the level of awareness of the working class. All Americans must be encouraged to study the most essential works of Marx and Lenin, to become card carrying members of the two parties, to become politically active, to attempt to take control of their lives. In short, they must prepare for the Dictatorship of the Proletariat.

We will know we are succeeding when the banners and posters read:

Workers of the World, Unite!
Scientific Socialism!
Dictatorship of the Proletariat!

8

APPEAL TO PROFESSIONAL PEOPLE

The impeachment of Donald Trump is over. It is officially a matter of history. The Senate has now given that man a blank check. He no longer has any restrictions placed on his authority. As a matter of celebration, he is now firing anyone and everyone whom he considers to be a threat to him. The journalists are now reporting that Trump is "weaponizing the presidency". Even anyone who could potentially be a threat is under attack. Trump is now living proof of the adage that "power corrupts. Absolute power corrupts absolutely". Donald Trump is no longer merely corrupt. Donald Trump is now absolutely corrupt.

This is not to say that the impeachment and subsequent trial of Trump was a mistake. It was not. It was absolutely the correct course of action. Countless working people, mainly members of the working class, proletarians, but also members of the middle class, petty bourgeois, demanded this. They thought it best to use the democratic process to remove a corrupt president from office. That democratic process is spelled out quite clearly in the Constitution, the law of the land. As loyal, patriotic citizens, these Americans performed their duty. They have every reason to be proud.

Things did not work out quite the way they had planned. Instead of being removed from office, Trump is more deeply entrenched. Now members of the administration, those whom he considers to be "enemies", are not only being fired, but also publicly humiliated. They are being escorted out of the White House by armed guards, as if they were common criminals. Their only "crime" is that of honouring summons, issued by the Congress. To ignore such a summons is a criminal act, which can result in charges of Contempt of Congress and considerable time in prison. They are being punished because they respect the law.

Such little details do not concern Trump. Journalists are reporting that Trump values loyalty above all else. That is true, as far as it goes. They are careful not to add that this loyalty is a one way street. Trump values loyalty to Trump. Trump has no loyalty to anyone else, with the possible exception of his immediate family. His loyalty, as well as the loyalty of all elected officials, should be to the Constitution they have all sworn to "preserve, protect and defend". The same can be said for the people who work for these elected officials. In the case of Trump, all such employees, those who are the slightest bit principled, are now receiving their walking papers.

This helps to simplify and clarify the class conflict. It is *not* to say that the proletariat, or at least the most advanced members of the proletariat, will be able to logically conclude that the class of monopoly capitalists, the bourgeoisie, are in power and must be overthrown. Such an expectation is simply not reasonable.

It is a fundamental tenet of Marxism that *the working class is not aware of itself as a class*. The conditions of life of the working class, the proletariat, do not lead to that awareness. That awareness can only come from an outside source, which is to say from a different class, the middle class, the petty bourgeois. Bear in mind that both Marx and Lenin were members of the middle class.

Now we are in the midst of a revolutionary situation, in that countless working people, those who were formerly apathetic, are now taking an interest in their lives. They are challenging the existing authority, demanding change, holding their democratically elected leaders accountable. That is a far cry from class consciousness. It is a big step in the right direction, but only a step. Without the awareness of themselves as a class, a class which is in conflict with the class of monopoly capitalists, the bourgeoisie, they cannot go any further.

That is where the members of the middle class come into play. Now it is up to class conscious people, and of course I am referring to Marxist intellectuals, those who are current or former members of the petty bourgeois, to step up and do their duty. The fact is that up until now, they have been sadly negligent.

I realize there are a great many people who will take offence to that statement. Yet I make no apologies. Certain things simply have to be done, just as certain things have to be said. Consider this a wake up call, because that is precisely the case. The proletariat is doing their best, rising up as they should, striking out wildly, if for no other reason than that they *lack leaders!*

No doubt there are many people who will object that the working people have no shortage of leaders. As proof, they will point to the crowded field of candidates who are currently competing to run for president, on behalf of the Democratic Party. In fact, as I write this, the primary "gong show" in the state of Iowa is now a thing of the past, while those same folks are now focused on New Hampshire. The journalists are having a joyous time reporting on the fighting among those candidates. Their only complaint is that there is not more insults being exchanged. They are having a difficult time distinguishing "tweedle dee from tweedle dum".

In fact, none of these candidates are leaders of the working class, for the plain and simple reason that none of them are Marxists. Whether they know it or not -and some of them do not- they all serve the same class, the bourgeoisie. *The political platform of each and every one of those candidates is completely acceptable to the bourgeoisie!*

That includes the platform of Bernie Sanders, the self proclaimed "independent socialist". Marx referred to such people as utopian socialists, and the sad fact is that all attempts at utopian socialism have been an abject failure. There is no reason to believe that the "independent socialism" of Bernie Sanders will fare any better. There is every reason to believe that the American bourgeoisie will crush any such attempt in the bud.

The fact of the matter is that *Marxists are the only leaders of the working class.* Only those who advocate the theories of

Marx and Lenin can truly refer to themselves as leaders of the working class. A true Marxist raises the level of awareness of the working class, focuses mainly upon the most advanced strata of the proletariat, as it is the most advanced workers who are deeply respected by the other workers. It is these advanced workers who must become advocates of the Dictatorship of the Proletariat, familiar with the most essential works of Marx and Lenin. *These advanced workers must be raised to the level of scientific socialists!*

Of course this is not happening, as the most advanced workers are not capable of becoming scientific socialists, if left to their own devices. And they are being left to their own devices. It is the role of leaders to provide that direction, and as yet, there is no Marxist political party in America. The parties which claim to be Marxist or Socialist do not call for the Dictatorship of the Proletariat, and that is the key "plank" in any party platform, that which separates the true Marxist party from the opportunist parties, those which merely claim to be Marxists. It is also absolutely not acceptable to the bourgeoisie, which is not a coincidence.

There is currently a desperate need for leaders, a Marxist political party to lead the working class. If it is not Marxist, then it is of necessity bourgeois, as there is no middle ground. As we live in a class society, that is just the way it is. It can be either Marxist, proletarian, or bourgeois.

The revolutionary motion is becoming ever more intense. Without doubt, it will soon break out into open warfare. Equally without doubt, when that happens the bourgeoise, or at least their loyal servants, boot lickers one and all, will attempt to take control of the revolution, to seize political power, to set themselves up as the new rulers. We must be prepared for that.

With that in mind, I can only suggest that Marxists come together and form a true Marxist political party, perhaps titled Communist Party, Dictatorship of the Proletariat, one which can lead the working class. I can also suggest that such a Party call for an alliance with all other Leftist parties and groups, those who claim to be Marxists as well as those who make no such claim. The groups Black Lives Matter, Me Too and the Democratic Socialists of America come to mind, although there are many others. As long as the true Marxist Party is careful to draw a clear distinction between them the other groups, I can see no problem. Of course, without such a distinction, such an alliance is out of the question.

The members of that admittedly temporary alliance should encourage all Americans to become politically active. Among other things, citizens should be advised to become card carrying members of the two mainstream political parties, Democratic and Republican. If they, along with their family and friends, join the two parties, then they will wield true political power. As "party bosses", they will be the people who determine any and all candidates to run for political office. They can choose the same person to run on behalf of both parties, including the office of the presidency. If nothing else, that should help to keep campaign expenses to a minimum.

To put this in context, it has just been reported that one contender for the presidency has already raised 350 million, and he has not taken part in even one political event, whether a primary state vote or a debate. It is facts such as these which

Marxists must use to drive home to the working class as examples of the power of capital.

As well, Americans should be advised to become active on a state and federal level, in the interests of abolishing the Electoral College. The only thing required is an amendment to the Constitution. A great many people are bitter over the fact that Hillary Clinton won the majority of the popular vote, yet lost the election. The only reason Trump is president is because of the archaic Electoral College, a College which was set up to protect the slave owners. Now it is being used to protect the bourgeoisie, including Trump. It is proper to stress the fact that citizens have the *right* to change the Constitution, if not the *duty* to force through such changes, when such changes are required. Now, with Trump occupying the White House, such a change is long overdue.

No doubt this Marxist political party will soon take shape, as the revolutionary motion causes even the most apathetic petty bourgeois intellectual to embrace the theories of Marx and Lenin. To such people I can only suggest communicating with working class people in a manner they can understand, without becoming condescending. Focus on the most advanced workers, using the scientific expressions followed by the more popular expressions. Bear in mind that we learned the alphabet through repetition. At the same time, more popular literature should be made available for the less advanced workers, as such workers should not be neglected. Be sure to avoid the use of all vulgarity. Make every effort to raise workers to a higher level. Under no circumstances stoop to the level of the least advanced.

The internet has provided us with a valuable tool. Feel free to take advantage of this. At the same time, try not to be a complete bore. The sad fact is that most socialist literature is just that, a bore. Most working people get tired of being told, over and over again, that which they already know. Face the fact that working people watch the news and further, they pay strict attention to the news. This is not to say that they completely understand the news, if only because the journalists present the analysis of current events as facts. They are not facts, merely opinions, even though they are stated as facts.

Perhaps the best way to educate people, to raise their level of awareness, is by focusing on current events, that which has the interest of working people, and doing so in a manner which is entertaining. The current political situation has the attention of people, and not just the impeachment of Trump. Use these events to drive home the point that Trump is not the problem. He is merely the most obvious symptom.

Also bear in mind that the working people pay strict attention to celebrities and professional people. They can be one and the same, but not always. They also listen closely to scientists.

No doubt attentive readers will suspect that is a none too subtle jab at the Hollywood people, and you are right. I use that term as a reference to the people who earn a living as actors, whether in movies or on television. I believe it is referred to as large screen and small screen, and matters to those members of the Hollywood set. My only concern is in using those people to raise the level of awareness of the working class. Their faces are immediately recognizable to all working people, and most of them are well loved. That especially applies to the females, the women who are exceptionally famous. For the most part, those are the same people who have been the most abused by the Hollywood executives. It would seem that the more famous the woman, the more the executives take delight in humiliating and degrading her.

These women have an added incentive to become active. Most of them are aware that there is no chance of charging these lowlifes, the executives who have made a career of assaulting women, if only because of the statute of limitations. To these women, I can only suggest that you "broaden your horizons", so to speak. Instead of seeking justice for assault by one member of the bourgeoisie, hold all members of the class accountable. Take action. Join the two parties. Encourage your family, friends and fans to do the same. I guarantee that your fans will listen to you. Then you and your fans can choose individuals to run for any and all political offices. That includes offices in the Congress, Senate and the Presidency, as well as state and local offices. Run for governor, for example, and make sure the same person runs for any and all offices as both Republican and Democratic. Become part of a nation wide movement to abolish the archaic Electoral College. Bear in mind that the Electoral College is the only reason Trump is in the White House.

At the same time, use your status as a celebrity to *make headlines!* You and your friends can carry posters and banners which call for revolution and the Dictatorship of the Proletariat. Disrupt the bourgeoisie at all times. Give them no peace. Harass them at these ridiculous debates, especially as that is the events which attract the attention of the press. Make it clear that as card carrying members of the two parties, you are determined that Sanders will run for president on behalf of both parties.

Carry banners and posters to the houses and offices of the bourgeoisie, to the fancy restaurants where they dine, to the clubs where they hire prostitutes and party. Join various groups and organizations and become part of the movement to overthrow the bourgeoisie. Take comfort in the fact that after the revolution, after the bourgeoisie are overthrown and crushed under the Dictatorship of the Proletariat, the statute of limitations will no longer apply. At that point, the lowlifes who assaulted you women will be held to account. What is more, they will not be allowed to hide behind a battery of lawyers. They will have to face a different set of judges, those who will be appointed by the working people, people such as yourself. Upon conviction, those creeps can expect to be sentenced to spending some quality time with the women they abused. It is up to you ladies to determine the punishment to mete out to them. Feel free to be creative.

Such happy thoughts may serve as an inspiration to the women who have been told they will never receive justice, due to one technicality or another. That may be true, but only under capitalism. Under the Dictatorship of the Proletariat, you will be guaranteed justice.

Not too long ago, the press quite cheerfully reported on the picketing and harassment of members of the Trump administration, among others. Then for some reason that died down, perhaps because people were focused on the impeachment and trial of Trump. It is to be hoped that such activity will flare up again, only now with more focus. No doubt the entertainers, to whom I am appealing, will come up with more creative ways of exposing the bourgeoisie. I have complete confidence in you. God Bless You!

As usual, I choose to end this article with my usual suggestions for slogans, those which I trust will soon become household expressions:

Workers of the World, Unite!
Scientific Socialism!
Dictatorship of the Proletariat!
Join the Two Parties!
Sanders For President!

9

APPEAL TO WOMEN

The impeachment and subsequent trial, by the Senate, of President Trump is now finished. The fall election, including the effort of Trump to win another four years in office as president, is now in full swing. The inconvenience of the trial is behind him, and he can now focus on his re-election, starting with the punishment of all of those who were guilty of the terrible crime of performing their democratic duty, against the wishes of their president. Those who respected the subpoena of the Congress and spoke the truth are now feeling the full wrath of the executive branch. As far as Trump is concerned, he is merely at the head of a huge company which has to do as he wishes.

At the same time, he is also rewarding those who have remained faithful to him. One of his old buddies, a first class boot licker, was recently convicted of numerous crimes, including perjury, in that he lied to Congress. The prosecutors in the case recommended a prison sentence of 7 to 9 years, and Trump is complaining that the sentence is too severe. He even had another of his old boot licking buddies, an individual whom he rewarded with a posting as Attorney

General, to interfere in the case. The four prosecutors on that case have quit the case in protest. It remains to be seen if Trump will fire them from their office. In addition, their boss, who was nominated for a top post at the Treasury Department, has now been denied that post. This is being referred to as an "existential threat" to the whole criminal justice system in the country. That is precisely the case. The morale within the Justice Department is at an all time low. Numerous other prosecutors are expected to hand in their resignations in protest. Even the presiding judge in the trial of the friend of Trump is being insulted. Even if his old buddy is sentenced, Trump may well grant him a presidential pardon. When asked if he would grant that pardon, Trump replied that he "would rather not say".

Now Trump is turning his attention to other unfinished business, that of starting a war with Iran. He is furious that the Senate has passed a resolution which limits his ability to go to war with Iran. In fact, eight Republican Senators joined the Democrats in passing that resolution. Now the resolution will go to the House of Representatives and very likely be passed. At that point it will go to Trump, and he will no doubt veto it. It will take a vote of two thirds of both houses of Congress to override that veto, which means that it will be necessary for twelve more Republican Senators to vote with the Democrats. That is not likely to take place, as they have collectively established themselves as a pack of gutless wonders.

Not that such a resolution should be necessary, as the Constitution makes it quite clear that only the Senate has the right to declare war. The last time America declared war was in 1941. The various wars the country has waged since that time have been instigated by the president, and Trump is determined to carry on that time honoured tradition. Trump has every intention of going to war with Iran.

In other news, the Democratic Party is also very busy. They are focused on the primaries, and in fact the only self proclaimed "democratic socialist", Senator Bernie Sanders, has fared quite well in the first two primaries. The press is following these primaries very closely, as the journalists are hoping that the Democrats can choose a candidate who can defeat Trump in November. They are speculating that Sanders is "too far to the Left", and are encouraging the Party to choose someone who is more "of a centrist". With that in mind, they are biased towards Senator Amy Klobuchar, Senator Elizabeth Warren or former Vice President Joe Biden. Then again, another member of the bourgeoisie, an individual who is reported to be every bit as rich as Donald Trump, by the name of Michael Bloomberg, is reported to be planning to "throw his hat into the ring", in time for Super Tuesday. Assuming he wins the nomination, then the American voters will be given the choice of one member or another of the bourgeoisie to rule over them.

For the moment, the candidates and the press are focused on the next two primaries, in Nevada and South Carolina, in the month of February. The big prize is not until March, when fourteen states decide their candidates on the day referred to as Super Tuesday.

As for those on the Left, Marxist and non Marxist, who are not concerned with these little details, I can only suggest that you are making a mistake. A great many members of the public, both working class and middle class, are closely watching these developments. They are looking for leaders, deeply dissatisfied with Trump, not sure of how to proceed. At best, they are trying to determine the best candidate for whom to vote.

It is up to conscious people, Marxists, to suggest to these people an alternative, or more accurately, an addition to voting. They can become card carrying members of the two parties, Democratic and Republican. They can choose their own candidates to run for office. They can demand the abolition of the Electoral College. It is not reasonable to expect working people to figure this out for themselves. It is up to class conscious people to explain to them the existence of classes and the conflict between the classes.

The best way to do this -if not the only way- is to encourage them in their struggles. As countless working people are now politically active, no longer apathetic, it is up to Leftist people, especially Marxists, to raise their level of awareness, to the level of scientific socialists, to Marxists. The most essential works of Marx and Lenin should be made available to them. Of course only the most advanced workers will become true Marxists, while we can expect a great many workers to become card carrying members of the parties. We can also expect these workers, card carrying members, party bosses, to nominate the people whom are most respected by those workers, to run for office. In other words, they will nominate the most advanced members of the working class to run for office. That is precisely the very thing we want. In the process of running for office and in trying to amend the Constitution, they will receive a most valuable education, training which will serve them in good stead after the revolution, after we establish the Dictatorship of the Proletariat. Such workers will be posted in key positions of authority.

On the one hand, we need a true political party to lead the working people, proletarians and petty bourgeois. I suggest the name Communist Party, Dictatorship of the Proletariat, CP, DP. I also suggest that this Party form an alliance with all Leftist parties and organizations, and in fact with all progressive people who are dissatisfied with the current political situation. That can include all former and current members of the Trump administration, as many of them are not at all happy. At the same time, the Marxist party must reserve the right to put forward their own political platform, as otherwise there is no basis for any alliance.

For the moment, the ridiculous debates and primary votes are providing the Leftist people with a fine opportunity to raise the level of awareness of the public. The journalists are focused on this, so feel free to give them something on which to report.

The fact is that women are leading the revolution, and they have proven themselves to be excellent organizers. Lately they have been rather quiet, but without doubt they can do again that which they did in the past, especially at the inauguration of Trump. Some such similar motion is required, but with more emphasis on class awareness. The point must be driven home to the working class that they are members of a class, the proletariat, a class which is at war with the class of monopoly capitalists, the bourgeoisie. People must carry posters and banners, filled with slogans which drive home the point.

There is no time to lose, as even the most die hard supporters of the bourgeoisie are worried, referring to the current political situation as a "perfect storm". They are even using the "R" word, which is to say revolution. Even they, loyal boot lickers of the bourgeoisie one and all, can see the revolutionary storm clouds gathering. Even though they are terrified, they cannot seem to decide on a course of action. This makes them completely unpredictable, more dangerous.

Some time ago, many members of the Trump administration vowed to stop Trump, "one way or another". For what ever reason, this has not happened. Precisely the opposite has taken place. The Senate has just given him unlimited power. He is now using that power as he sees fit. For the moment, he is focused on punishing those whom he views as enemies, while rewarding others for their service to him, not for their service to their country.

Now is the time to march, but with goals which are broader than that of opposing Trump. Now the ultimate goal must be to raise the level of awareness of the proletariat, to overthrow the bourgeoisie and establish the Dictatorship of the Proletariat. March across the country, to the homes and offices of the capitalists, to their vacation areas, to their debates and voting stations. Give them no peace. Now they are divided, at their weakest, and the working people are aroused, working class and middle class united. Now is the time to strike, with the two classes, proletariat and petty bourgeois at their strongest.

It is asking a great deal, but you have done it in the past and you can do it again. Perhaps all previous revolutions have been led by men, but just because a revolution has never been led by women does not mean it cannot be done. Now is the time to make history, to prove that a woman can do any job a man can do. That includes leading a revolution. God Bless You, One And All.

I will close with my usual slogans, which I can suggest for the banners and posters.

Workers of the World, Unite!
Scientific Socialism!
Dictatorship of the Proletariat!

10

FORM AN AMERICAN INDEPENDENT CITIZENS SOCIETY

The impeachment and trial by Senate of President Donald Trump is now officially a matter of history. He has been acquitted of all charges, even though the Speaker of the House, Nancy Pelosi, maintains that as there were no witnesses and no evidence presented at the trial, he was not acquitted. Her capacity for self delusion is quite impressive. No doubt a great many Americans are questioning the qualifications of a politician who occupies such an important post as Speaker of the House. Such an individual should have the ability to face reality, regardless of the unpleasantness of that reality.

The fear now, at least among Americans with a considerable education, is that the American empire will follow in the footsteps of the Roman Empire. For the benefit of those who are just now becoming politically active, I will point out that the Roman Empire started out as a republic, which is to say that it was ruled by a Senate, and did not recognize any monarch. This is not to say that it was a democratic republic, because it was not. The common people were not in charge. The aristocracy appointed members of their own to the Senate, and it was the Senate which was in charge.

Without going into detail, that situation changed when an ambitious general decided to take power. As the troops under his command were loyal to him, not to the Empire, he was able to set himself up as emperor, referred to as Caesar. The Roman Senate either could not or would not stop him, and the Empire ceased to be a republic. By definition, a republic does not recognize a monarch. The Roman Empire was transformed into a monarchy, Caesar had unlimited power, used it accordingly, and the Empire quickly fell into decline.

The current situation is a bit more complex, in that Trump is not a general, even though he is the Commander in Chief of the American military. Still, it is doubtful that he has the support of the military. At least, the military has no reason to place their loyalty to their Commander in Chief, above that of the Constitution they have sworn to protect and defend. Trump humiliates and ridicules the military at every opportunity. For that matter, Trump humiliates and ridicules anyone and everyone as he sees fit, especially if they disagree with him. Even though Trump is not a member of the nobility, he has the mentality of the nobility. No wonder he plans to set himself up as an American emperor!

The American Senate has now just "paved the road" for Trump, in that they have voted to acquit. The "trial" of Trump consisted of little more than the formality of a vote, preceded by various arguments. The one and only government body with the Constitutional authority to curb the power of the president has effectively abdicated that authority, thereby granting the president unlimited power.

As that is the case, it is now up to American citizens to take action. The constitutional process, that of checks and balances between the various branches of government, is not working. The legislative branch is no longer keeping the executive branch in check. The trial has taught Trump a valuable lesson. He now knows that he can do anything he wants.

In response to this, I can only suggest that Americans who are concerned with the current state of affairs set up an American Independent Citizens Society. Such a Society must by definition be non profit, so that the capitalists cannot hijack the organization as they did the Womens protest group of several years ago. It should be legally established, with the goal of protecting and defending the democratic republic, as outlined in the American Constitution.

That should appeal to Americans from all walks of life, working class and middle class. In the interests of achieving their stated goal of defending and protecting the democratic republic, the members of the Society can be encouraged to become card carrying members of the two parties, Democratic and Republican. They can also be encouraged to become politically active on a local, state and federal level. As party bosses, they can nominate candidates to run for political office. They can also be part of a "grass roots" movement to amend the Constitution, to abolish the electoral college. In this way the democratic republic will remain a republic, while making it more democratic, in that the majority of voters will determine the next president. In addition, the influence of capital will be reduced.

Of course, members of the Society can also be members of other organizations, whether it is of a church, synagogue, temple, trade union, sports club or political party, among others. The religious and political beliefs of individuals should be kept separate from the goals of the Society. In this way, those who are "right wing" can come together with those who are "Leftist", pro life can unite with pro choice, atheists can unite with Evangelicals, Marxist can unite with Anarchists and Revisionists, liberals and conservatives will be on speaking terms, gun control advocates will sit with members of the NRA, and lo and behold, the sun will continue to shine. Those who delight in chaos and confusion, the monopoly capitalists, the bourgeoisie, will gaze in awe and wonder, weeping and wailing, crying out in the depths of despair, praying to the gods of the underworld, in mortal dread of this challenge to their authority.

Indeed, such a Society is a challenge to their authority. The bourgeoisie is in charge, and they fully intend to remain in charge. They are very few in number but extremely wealthy. The ideology of the bourgeoisie is wide spread, if only because they control the press. Their propaganda is continuous and effective, and must be opposed. They thrive on dissent and confusion.

In this way, the various political parties in the country, including the soon to be formed Communist Party, Dictatorship of the Proletariat, can continue to call for revolution and the subsequent Dictatorship of the Proletariat. Of course, other parties and organizations can also put forward their political platform, as they see fit. As long as this is kept separate from the work of the Society, there can be no problem.

Gerald McIsaac

The revolutionary motion currently taking place has given birth to countless citizens who are anxious to become politically active. At the same time, many of them are understandably confused. Different political parties and organizations say different things, and they cannot all be correct. The formation of a Society with the stated goal of protecting and defending the Constitution should appeal to all members of the public, or at least to the vast majority of people, those who are honest, tax paying citizens.

These citizens will in turn learn, if only from bitter experience, that the bourgeoisie are in charge and fully intend to remain in charge. Those who are not yet class conscious will soon become class conscious. They will also learn that the Marxists are correct, that it is necessary to overthrow the dictatorship of the bourgeoisie and replace it with the Dictatorship of the Proletariat. This Dictatorship can only be achieved through revolution. The training these honest citizens receive will serve as valuable training, as after the revolution, such workers can and will be placed in key positions of authority.

Now it is up to progressive people, whether working class or middle class, scientists, scholars, intellectuals or merely people who want to make a difference, to form such a society. It will merely require a little time and effort, and the rewards will be immense. I fully expect this Society to be soon established, and further expect it to be formed by the same people who did such a fine job of organizing the womens march of several years ago. The difference this time will be that the capitalists will not be able to hijack the movement. Then too, this Society will be even finer and stronger.

11

THE CRISIS INTENSIFIES

The two farces of the Democratic Presidential primaries, that of New Hampshire and Iowa, are now a thing of the past. The next two farces, that of Nevada and South Carolina, are currently in full swing. The press is focused on the Democratic Presidential Debates and the numerous candidate who are determined to win the Party nomination and challenge Trump for the political jackpot, that of the presidency. Even though it is early in the election, they have already collectively spent hundreds of millions of dollars. The one candidate who has yet to run in even one primary is reported to have spent, or at least raised, over *400 million*, and this in a country with massive unemployment, millions of people on food stamps, countless people living on the streets, and millions scraping by as best they can. Perhaps someone should mention to these politicians that all of those millions could better be spent elsewhere.

This in no way changes the fact that the press is covering these primaries and a great many people are watching, and in fact the members of the public are paying strict attention. Most people, both working class and middle class, are deeply dissatisfied with the current state of events, and are seeking an alternative. In other words, they are looking for leaders. Most of them are disappointed, but not surprised that none of the candidates are offering any substantial alternative. The only candidate who offers anything even slightly different is Bernie Sanders, a self described Independent Socialist. Of course, voters are torn between a candidate whom they like, and of course I am referring to Sanders, and a candidate who has the best chance of beating Trump. The press is stressing the point that Sanders may be a fine fellow, but as he is not a "centrist", he does not have any broad support and therefore has no chance of beating Trump. This is their opinion and they state it frequently, as if it is a fact. It is not a fact, it is an opinion, and should be stated as such. It is also very likely not true.

Most members of the middle class have been ruined, forced into the ranks of the working class, so that there are essentially only two classes in America, the working class, the proletariat, and the monopoly capitalists, the bourgeoisie. There is no middle class and consequently no middle ground, no centre. Most members of the press, the journalists, either cannot or will not face this fact. As the companies they work for are owned by the capitalists, they are forced to bias the news they report, in favour of the bourgeoisie. Otherwise, they find themselves in the ranks of the unemployed. Or perhaps, as supremely well paid people, they cannot imagine an alternative to capitalism. They may even qualify as members of the middle class, petty bourgeois. That is an academic question, best left to the political scientists. It is a question to which I am indifferent.

A far more interesting development is that the journalists are now using words which were formerly forbidden, such as "revolution" and "socialism". The fact that they are now openly referring to such topics is an indication of the strength of the revolutionary motion, that which is currently gripping the country.

Other topics are in the news, and the working people closely watch the news. Among the most remarkable is the reports that 1100 federal judges are about to convene an emergency meeting, over concerns about Department of Justice interventions in politically sensitive cases. Not that it is the DOJ which is interfering in such cases so much as it is Trump ordering his Attorney General to meddle. In particular, he is quite upset that his old buddy, Roger Stone, was convicted of various crimes and could be sentenced to several years in prison, in fact seven to nine years, as is recommended by the prosecution. Trump wants to change this, and is insulting the prosecutors and the judge on the case. The Attorney General is complaining but doing as he is told. In turn, over 2,000 current or former members of the office of the AG, have called for him to resign.

It is doubtful that the AG will resign for this reason, just as it is doubtful that the federal judges will be able to take any meaningful action. The important thing to note is that the members of the administration are deeply divided. The judicial branch, which was set up by the bourgeoisie, as part of the state apparatus used to protect the bourgeoisie and crush the proletariat, is now in disarray, quarrelling with the executive branch. The ruling class is truly divided, deeply weakened.

Another leader of the working class, Angelina Ocasio-Cortez, is also in the news. She is reported to have said that "Sanders may have to nix his medicare for all plan". Such a statement reveals that she is indeed naive, very childish -a good thing if she is only naive! There is no way that the monopoly capitalists are about to allow Sanders or anybody else to interfere with their profits. No doubt, there are greater profits to be made in other areas, other than taking advantage of the suffering of people, but none come to mind. All dope dealers can testify to the fact that the profits are huge.

No sooner will we be through the primary farces of February, than we will be faced with the major farce of "Super Tuesday" in March. It is expected that another presidential candidate, Michael Bloomberg, will be "throwing his hat into the ring" at that time, if not sooner. As he has already spent hundreds of millions on the campaign, this should come as no surprise. The press is already reporting allegations of racism and sexual assault. As he is a billionaire, a member of the monopoly capitalist class, the bourgeoisie, this should not come as a great shock to anyone. Such people tend to view women as members of a harem, to be used accordingly. This should be used to drive home the point that Trump is no different from any other member of his class. In other words, all members of the bourgeoisie are completely reactionary.

As I write this, it has just been reported that Trump has just issued pardons for Rod Blagojevich and ten others. The significance of this is that Blagojevich was the former governor of Illinois, in office at the time Barrack Obama was elected president. As Obama was a Senator from Illinois, he had to relinquish his Senate seat, and it was up to the governor to appoint a new Senator. Blagojevich saw this as an opportunity to sell the Senate seat to the highest bidder, and apparently he was conducting the auction on the telephone. Of course, the FBI was recording the call. This is not too surprising, as Illinois is the home state of Capone, among other notable criminals. It is considered to be perhaps the most corrupt state in the union, with possibly four of the last seven governors ending up in prison. The fact that Blagojevich advertised the sale on the telephone is a testament to his stupidity. No self respecting professional criminal would do something that stupid. So of course Trump issued him a pardon, as he probably identifies with Blagojevich. One is as stupid as the other.

These are headlines from the latest news, and the Leftist people should be using these as examples to drive home the point that classes exist and are in constant conflict. That is the only way the working class can be made aware of themselves as a class. As the revolution could break out any day now, the need to raise the level of awareness of the working class, the proletariat, is ever more pressing. The fact that even federal judges are concerned is an indication of the breadth and depth of the movement.

The fact is that these primaries and debates are pure nonsense, noise created with the obvious purpose of deceiving the people and *extinguishing the growing revolution* by diverting the attention of the people onto trivial matters.

Now is the time for American women to once again rise up, to come together as you did at the time Trump was inaugurated. Also avoid the trap of allowing the movement to be converted into a corporation. Instead, set up a non profit society, one which can appeal to all citizens. Encourage all

Americans to join the two parties and take part in amending the Constitution, abolishing the Electoral College. The only thing required is the vote of two thirds of the states. As well, encourage the members to nominate people for all political offices. Flood Washington and all state capitals with Leftist people.

In addition, those of you who are Marxists *must* form a Communist Party, Dictatorship of the Proletariat. The revolution needs leaders. As conscious people, it is your duty. Not to perform your duty is completely unprincipled, the basest form of opportunism.

This can still be accomplished before the November elections. American women, perhaps in cooperation with American students, have proven themselves to be excellent organizers. They have done it in the past and can do so again. The only thing they lack is leaders. It would appear that the leaders of the Womens Protest of several years ago have sold out to the bourgeoisie. Or perhaps they have merely decided to remain silent. Either way, that is not acceptable.

Other leaders will emerge in the struggle, either before or after the revolution. You ladies know who you are, so step up and take charge. If you do not, a member of the bourgeoisie will do that for you. Then everything you have fought for will be in vain.

The Independent Citizens Society should be open to all Americans, dedicated to protecting and defending the democratic republic, the Constitution. That should appeal to all, including the federal judges who are so dissatisfied. The deeper and broader the base, the better. We want to gather together as many citizens as possible.

By contrast, the CP, DP must be very exclusive. Only the most dedicated, seasoned Marxists can be allowed to join. It is this Party, the one and only true Party of the working class, which can possibly lead the revolution to socialism and the subsequent Dictatorship of the Proletariat.

The fate of the American revolution is in the hands of American women. I have no doubt that you will rise to the occasion. God Bless You.

12

BLOOMBERG AND THE DEMOCRATIC PRIMARIES

The Las Vegas Democratic presidential debate is now behind us, and one more political farce is a bit of history. The capitalists are doing their best to divert the revolutionary movement, using these "debates" and "town halls" as "smoke and mirrors" to distract the working class, if you will excuse the metaphor. Such metaphors must be used, in order to raise the level of awareness of the working class, the proletariat, to the level of Marxists. At least, the most advanced members of the proletariat must become class conscious, as the less advanced have the utmost respect for such people. It is up to middle class intellectuals, either current or former members of that class, to bring this class awareness to the proletariat. With that in mind, feel free to use metaphors, especially sports metaphors, as most working people are familiar with sports. Also, repetition of the scientific terms, as we all learned the alphabet through repetition. Try to communicate with people in an entertaining manner, as most political articles are a crashing bore.

Bear in mind that the revolutionary motion is in "high gear", which means that countless people, those whom were formerly apathetic, are now rising up, taking an interest in politics, determined to make a difference, looking for leaders and disappointed in the current crop of candidates for the presidency. Who can blame them?

This in no way changes the fact that the working people, members of the public, both proletariat and middle class, are closely watching those political spectacles. As that is the case, it is up to class conscious people, and especially Marxists, to use these as examples to help raise the level of awareness of the public. I can further suggest avoiding the use of the word masses, as most people find the word rather offensive. Such people tend to refer to themselves as common people, or rank and file.

The latest debate in Las Vegas, in preparation for the Nevada primary, was entertaining, if nothing else. The journalists are reporting "sparks flying", and one of them, an individual whom has managed to maintain his sense of humour -one of the few-compared this to "Titanic meeting the iceburg", in that Bloomberg was the Titanic and Senator Elizabeth Warren was the iceburg. Well done! Now if only Leftist writers could learn to communicate in that manner.

The journalists are also quite gleefully reporting that Bloomberg is worth *60 billion*, so that he is one of the richest men in the world, and not just America. He was formerly the mayor of New York City, and used the police tactic of "stop and frisk" against "visible minorities", which is to say "people of colour", either Afro American or Hispanic, otherwise known as "black or brown". He is reported to have endorsed "redlining", and is considered to be a racist and a misogynist, which is likely true, just as it is true that most common people are not aware of the meaning of the word misogynist.

Most people are aware of the meaning of the word racist, and misogyny is nothing more than prejudice against women. Then again, some people distinguish between sexists, those who are prejudiced against women, and misogynists, as those who are even more despicable. Apparently Bloomberg is one of the more despicable.

It is such terms which should be explained to working people, if only because it has their attention.

In fact, Warren was quick to point out that numerous women had accused Bloomberg of sexual assault, and he had "paid them off", in that he had given them cash in return for signing a "non disclosure agreement", or "NDA". She further suggested that he should release those women from such an agreement, and of course he refused. This is not to say that Warren is necessarily the brightest of the presidential candidates, just that she has the best handlers.

It is notable that one of the candidates accused Sanders, a self described "Independent Socialist", of believing that "capitalism is the root of all evil". It should be pointed out to working people that this is one of the favourite tricks of the capitalists, or at least of their supporters, to accuse someone else of believing that which they know to be true!

It is an over simplification to say that "capitalism is the root of all evil", but as we live in a class society, it is not much of a stretch. Of course the candidate who accused Sanders of believing this also believes this, just as the capitalists believe this, but are not about to admit it, just as they are not about to deny it. This is a fine example of "moving to the centre", otherwise known as "straddling the fence", and should be pointed out to the working class.

The same candidate who made that accusation, against Sanders, also accused Bloomberg of thinking that "money is the root of all power". As Bloomberg is extremely wealthy, a member of the bourgeoisie, that is very likely also true. He very likely does believe this, and as we live under capitalism, we can all see his point. All working people can testify to the fact that money is power!

The fact that Bloomberg is being put forward as a candidate for president, as an alternative to Trump, is significant. Both are members of the same class, the bourgeoisie, and one is every bit the racist and sexist as is the other. Bloomberg does not even have his name on the ballot in Nevada, yet participated in the Las Vegas debate. The fact that this makes no sense is an indication that the bourgeoisie is desperate, unsure of how to proceed.

Bloomberg and Trump are members of the same class, the bourgeoisie, and could be twins. One is every bit as sexist and racist as the other, completely devoid of principle, technically referred to as opportunists. In other words, they are typical members of the bourgeoisie, completely reactionary. These are more technical terms with which the working class must become familiar.

No doubt the bourgeoisie, the ruling class, is worried. They are aware of the revolutionary movement which is sweeping the country, and are doing their best to combat this, to divert it onto some harmless motion for paltry reforms. Even though the journalists are using such words as revolution and socialism -words which were formerly forbidden- the word "secession" is still not allowed to be used.

The journalists are supremely well aware that the country is deeply divided, about to break apart, but are not allowed to say this. They are professional people with their "ear to the ground", so that they listen carefully to that which common people are saying. They are well aware that, for example, the state of California is close to breaking apart, and may form as many as five separate states, possible separating from the union. The state of Texas may also secede, and numerous other states are making similar "noises".

Without doubt, secession is merely a step upon the road to socialism, as to separate from a capitalist country to form another capitalist country is merely to "go from the frying pan into the fire". The very act of secession will provide people with a feeling of empowerment, which is precisely what it is, and they will then take the next step of overthrowing their capitalists and establishing a socialist society, in the form of the Dictatorship of the Proletariat. As that is the worst night mare of every capitalist, there is a good reason for their concern.

In the mean time, the capitalists are trying to focus the attention of the public on the primaries and "town hall meetings". Trump has the bright idea of encouraging the voters to vote in any and all state Democratic primaries, regardless of the party to which they are registered, in an effort to confuse the issue and hopefully block the nomination of Sanders.

As voting is part of the democratic process, I think that is a fine idea. The more people who become politically active, if only on the level of exercising their democratic right to vote, the better. That is at least a place to start.

As I write this, the journalists are also reporting that an old "associate" of Trump, Roger Stone, is being sentenced, much to the irritation of Trump. He personally interfered in the case to the point of insulting the prosecutors, the jury and even the judge. The prosecutors resigned in protest, the Attorney General bowed down to Trump and recommended a lighter sentence than the one which was recommended by the prosecutors. But now the newly appointed prosecutors are recommending the original sentence, as they maintain that a "substantial period of incarceration is appropriate". It is also reported that the judge tends to agree with the stiff sentence, if only because Stone was convicted of witness tampering, in that he threatened witnesses. As she just passed down a sentence of forty months, which is considerably less than that which the prosecutors recommended, but far more than the defence called for, it is clear that she too is defying Trump.

The fact that the new set of prosecutors have stood up to the Attorney General, and by extension Trump, is significant. As well, the federal judge is also holding her ground. It is an indication of the strength of the revolutionary motion.

No doubt there are many Leftist people, including Marxists, who are of the opinion that such little details as debates, town halls and court cases, are not worth discussing. They may want to focus on revolution and socialism. To such people I can only respond that we must "play the hand we are dealt". It is a fundamental tenet of Marxism that the working class must emancipate themselves. The well meaning members of the middle class cannot do this for the working class. Instead, it is up to middle class intellectuals to bring to the working class the awareness of themselves as a class, to raise their level of awareness to that of the level of conscious people, that of Marxists. The best way to do this -if not the only way- is to explain to the working people, in words they can understand, on subjects which concern them, the facts that classes exist and are in constant conflict. We do not get to choose the issues which are of concern to the proletariat. These issues can only serve as particulars, examples of the conflict between the classes. Marxists must use the particulars as examples to drive home the general.

Another particular is the fact that Trump can, and likely will, pardon Stone, regardless of the sentence which the judge hands down, which we now know is that of forty months in prison. This can be used to drive home the point that the judicial system is part of the state apparatus, which was set up to protect and serve the ruling class, the bourgeoisie. The laws do not apply to the capitalists, merely the working people. It is part of their method of rule. Regardless of what they say, the bourgeoisie are indeed "above the law".

It is my most fervent hope that a great many members of the working class will read this little article. As well, I am hoping that many middle class intellectuals will also take note. I have deliberately used various metaphors, which almost everyone can understand. I am also hoping that such intellectuals will carry the message in much the same manner.

On that subject, the American women in particular have proven themselves to be excellent organizers. I was deeply impressed, just as I was impressed by the same skills of the students. May I suggest that you form an alliance, of women and students, and do it again. We can only hope that a great many men join the cause. May I further suggest the goals of flooding the two mainstream political parties with Leftist people, as card carrying members, and of passing a Constitutional amendment to abolish the Electoral College. Past experience has proven, beyond any shadow of a doubt, that you can do this, almost immediately, even before the fall elections. Assuming that is the case, it will make these fool primary debates completely pointless.

That fact alone may serve as an inspiration. May I suggest that marches and demonstrations should carry banners and slogans which read:

Abolish the Electoral College!
Join the Two Parties!
Workers of the World, Unite!
Scientific Socialism!
Dictatorship of the Proletariat!

13

SANDERS AS FRONT RUNNER

Now that the Las Vegas presidential debate is a thing of the past - Thank God for minor mercies!- the journalists are reporting that Bernie Sanders is the clear front runner. They report this in a spirit of despair, as if the day of the debate should be considered a day of mourning. They report that Mike Bloomburg is of the opinion that the only winner of the debate was Donald Trump. Of course they report this as if it is a fact, rather than the opinion of one man. They neglect to report that the only loser of the debate was the American public.

The journalists also report that the "rivals of Sanders question his chances against Trump, as he is a socialist". Whether it is true or not, the main concern of the "rivals" is the fact that Sanders is not only an honest man, but a self described Independent Socialist. The very word "socialist" terrifies them, just as it terrifies all capitalists.

Even though Sanders is not a scientific socialist, a Marxist, but a utopian socialist, it makes no difference to the capitalists. It is entirely possible that they cannot distinguish between the two. As far as they are concerned, it may merely mean a different shade of the same colour, in this case red, and must be destroyed.

The fact of the matter is that only the Marxists are a real threat to the capitalists, the bourgeoisie, as only the Marxists are prepared to crush the vermin under the Dictatorship of the Proletariat, immediately after the revolution. But as the monopoly capitalists, referred to as imperialists, are completely reactionary, that is of no consequence. Any threat to their wealth and power will absolutely not be tolerated.

Of course the journalists are in the pay of the capitalists, and must, of necessity, slant the news in favour of the capitalists. If they do not, they will certainly receive their walking papers. Still, a certain amount of honesty manages to sneak through. The current mayor of New York City was interviewed and he quite cheerfully reported that most common people, or at least members of the Democratic Party, are quite excited about the prospect of having Sanders run against Trump in the fall election. This is in direct contradiction to the polls which the journalists see fit to quote, polls which, quite frankly, make no sense. The fact is that support for Sanders is growing, and the opposition from the capitalists is becoming ever stronger.

The bourgeois line is that someone who claims to be a socialist, even an Independent Socialist, has no chance of beating Trump. The very word "socialist" is something of an insult, a curse to be hurled at an opponent. The only Democratic candidate who has any chance of defeating Trump and becoming president must be a moderate, in order to appeal to the more moderate members of the Democratic

Party. So sayeth the political strategists of the Democratic Party.

It is clear that the political strategists have lost touch with reality, assuming they had any passing acquaintance with the old girl in the first place. There can be no thought of appealing to the more moderate members of the Democratic Party, as they no longer exist. Those who used to be considered as moderate have come to their senses and moved to the Left, attracted to Sanders and his brand of Democratic Socialism. This is clear from the reports of polls across the country, and especially the polls taken in the "Super Tuesday" states, to use the common expression. In short, support for Sanders and Independent Socialism is growing. Many Americans are now of the opinion that the one and only candidate who can beat Trump, is Bernie Sanders. That is the last thing the capitalists want to hear.

That is precisely the news that Marxists want to hear. This is not to say that the election of Sanders to the presidency will result in a socialist society, because it will not. It is very unlikely that the capitalists, the bourgeoisie, will allow Sanders to become president. From a Marxist viewpoint, the important thing is that the level of awareness of the members of the public is rising, the revolutionary motion is growing, becoming ever more intense. People are spontaneously gravitating to socialism. Our goal now is to flood Washington and all state capitals with Leftist people.

This may not be as far fetched as it sounds. The only thing required is that the women and students, those whom have proven themselves to be such excellent organizers, get into motion once again. They can form a society and once again march, calling for all Americans to join the two mainstream political parties, as card carrying members, and also call for the abolition of the Electoral College. They can also disrupt the "town halls" and "presidential debates", demanding to be heard, as is their democratic right. They can march to the houses and offices of the politicians and bureaucrats, carrying signs and banners, as they have in the past. Marching on the fancy restaurants and disrupting their meals has proven to be an effective tactic, and we hope to see more of this. This results in some fine press coverage, helping to raise the level of awareness of the working class. The members of The Squad must not be neglected. No doubt they are feeling like a minority. As they form the proletarian headquarters in Washington, there is a reason for this. They are a minority, under great pressure, and deserve our support. Let them know they are not alone, and will soon receive massive reinforcements. In fact, soon they will be members of the majority.

As elections for all members of Congress are held every two years, there is no reason to believe that Leftist people cannot conduct a massive campaign, in all fifty states, to first flood the two parties with Leftist people. Such card carrying members, party bosses, can in turn nominate candidates for office on behalf of both parties. That includes the presidency. It matters not if those people go to Washington as Republicans or Democrats. Mind you, the capitalists are sure to take a dim view of this.

The bourgeoisie are in charge and fully intend to remain in charge. That point must be driven home to the working class, but not by the citizens who are taking part in the revolution. The organization I am suggesting, which will no doubt be led by women and students, must be as broad based as possible. It must appeal to citizens of all political persuasions, socialists, anarchists, democrats, social democrats, republicans and communists, members of all religious beliefs and people of no religious belief, those who are pro life and those who are pro choice, gun control advocates and NRA members, and so on. Only such a union of Americans, the vast majority of Americans, can overthrow the bourgeoisie.

That stands in stark contrast to the party of the working class I am proposing. As there is only one working class, there can be only one party to represent that class. That party must be Marxist, as only Marxists serve the working class. With that in mind, I am suggesting the name Communist Party, Dictatorship of the Proletariat, or CP, DP.

In this way we can distinguish ourselves from the other parties which claim to be socialist or Marxist. As they disavow the Dictatorship of the Proletariat, they are clearly not Marxist. They are revisionists, and the political platform of such parties is perfectly acceptable to the bourgeoisie. The Dictatorship of the Proletariat is absolutely not acceptable to the bourgeoisie.

Such a party must, of necessity, be numerically very small. The importance lies not in the size of the party, but of the revolutionary line. It has to serve the people. It has to raise the level of awareness of the working class, so that at least the most advanced workers will become true Marxists.

That is where the middle class intellectuals come into play. Bear in mind that both Marx and Lenin were middle class, and make no mistake, they were intellectuals. It is only such people, or perhaps working class intellectuals who have been exposed to the revolutionary theories of Marx and Lenin, who can form the true Communist Party. To such people, I can only suggest that you step up and perform your duty.

As part of raising the level of awareness of the working class, be sure to make it quite clear that capitalism has been restored in both Russia and China, at least temporarily. Also make it clear that many of us believe in God, while others do not. To each his own.

Now that almost everyone has computers and the internet, as well as various digital devices, it is so much easier to carry the message. The days of leaflets are a thing of the past. No conscious person, by whom I am of course referring to Marxists, has any excuse for not being active in raising the level of awareness of the proletariat.

At the same time, try not to be too much of a bore. People get tired of being told that which they already know. They know they are struggling, trying to make ends meet. There is no need to rub their faces in it. Instead, focus on that which does concern them, and I am not talking about professional sports. Instead, if they are paying attention to the fact that Sanders is running for president, suggest that they support Sanders in this noble objective, while at the same time expressing the Marxist belief that the capitalists will never allow a peaceful transition to socialism.

The revolutionary motion is growing in intensity and could break out any day. If that happens, we will not have to worry about flooding Washington with Leftist people. We will be faced with a whole new set of challenges. We should be so lucky!

I will close this article with my usual suggestions for banners and posters, slogans which soon will become very popular:

Workers of the World, Unite!
Scientific Socialism!
Dictatorship of the Proletariat!

14

UNIONS AGAINST SANDERS

The Nevada Democratic presidential primary is very close, and the press is quite gleefully reporting that a very powerful union in the state is opposed to the nomination of Senator Sanders, a self described Democratic Socialist. They further report that it is a very big, powerful union with possibly 60,000 members. Apparently they fought for years to get an excellent medical coverage package, as part of their contract. This is no doubt true, as the capitalists are "reluctant" to provide medical coverage for their workers. More accurately, it is safe to say that the capitalists would sooner crawl on their bellies over broken glass, rather than spend any money, on medical coverage or anything else, for the benefit of their workers. Now apparently the union, or at least the union leaders, are afraid that if Sanders is elected president, his "medicare for all" will be a threat to their hard won medical insurance package.

It is very likely that the press is trying to drive a wedge between the unions and socialists, or at least Marxists. The reason for this is not clear, but the fact remains that there are a great many people who take great delight in causing trouble, spreading confusion, even though they have nothing to gain from these actions. No doubt the capitalists would love to see the "Left", go to war with the unions. Bear in mind that the word "Left" is a broad term I use in reference to the people who are fighting for the working people, both working class and middle class. That is not about to happen. But as the issue has been raised, it is best to face it.

Lenin had a few words to say concerning the trade unions, in that he placed the role of the trade unions in the proper perspective. As this is so instructive, I have quoted it at length. Lenin gave a speech on December 30, 1920, three years after the successful socialist revolution. He stated quite clearly, "Trade unions are not just historically necessary; they are historically inevitable as an organization of the industrial proletariat, and under the Dictatorship of the Proletariat, embrace nearly the whole of it…a school of administration, a school of economic management, a school of communism… what has necessarily come down to us from capitalism, and what comes from the ranks of the advanced revolutionary detachments, which you might call the revolutionary vanguard of the proletariat."

Rather than regarding the trade unions as competition for political power, it is correct to regard them as schools of communism, schools which were forced upon the proletariat by the capitalists, schools which train the revolutionary vanguard of the proletariat. It is the *duty* of all Leftist people, especially Marxists, to work as closely as possible with the trade unions. It is to their credit that they have expanded from the industrial proletariat to embrace workers in all branches of industry. Of course the capitalists do not know it, but they are "training" workers, preparing them for the approaching revolution and the subsequent Dictatorship of the Proletariat.

Lenin went into this in more detail in his excellent work, Left Wing Communism, An Infantile Disorder. He made it clear that unions "educate and school people, give them *all round development and an all round* training, so that they *are able to do anything.*" (italics by Lenin) He went on to explain that the proletariat was forced to form trade unions by the capitalists, and that in the most highly developed industrialized countries, the upper stratum of the proletariat has been bribed. As a result of this, a part of the upper stratum of the proletariat is not revolutionary, but in the service of the bourgeoisie. Some of these class traitors can be found in the trade unions. They are able to exercise their influence and are responsible for certain reactionary tendencies. One of the finest union leaders, Daniel De Leon, referred to them as "labour lieutenants of the capitalist class".

At the time of the Russian revolution of 1917, a great many people became politically active. Those whom had formerly been apathetic were roused to a fury, and especially in the case of the younger generation, many of them moved too far to the "Left". They refused to work in "reactionary trade unions"! This was a serious mistake, as the workers in the unions tend to be more advanced, even if some of their leaders are class traitors. To refuse to work among the unions is to drive those union members, the rank and file, into the ranks of the capitalists.

We can expect a similar situation to develop in America, possibly even before the revolution. As a grandparent, I can testify to the fact that youngsters in their teens invariably come to the conclusion that we are a bunch of old fools. It is only later in life, possibly as soon as they graduate from those teen years, that they are invariably amazed at just how much we have learned in such a short time! No doubt all grandparents have experienced something similar.

When a similar uprising of the youth happens here, as it most certainly will, we must welcome it. No doubt many young people, and some who are not so young, will lash out at people whom they perceive to be enemies, agents of the capitalists. While there is no shortage of such people, some working people have merely been misled. To attack these misguided workers, those who are perhaps less advanced, is a serious mistake. This is referred to as moving too far to the Left, and working in the service of the capitalists.

The fact of the matter is that the capitalists, the bourgeoisie, must be overthrown. It is also a fact that pure hatred, righteous indignation, is the "beginning of all wisdom", the basis of all socialist and communist movement and of its success. It is not enough. It is also necessary to train workers, to raise their level of awareness to that of conscious people, Marxists, to transform them into *proletarian* politicians. The working class needs leaders. In no other way can the bourgeoisie be defeated.

With that in mind, I can only stress the fact that we can learn from the experience of other revolutions, or we can repeat their mistakes. The previous revolution which most closely matches our own is the Russian revolution, led by Lenin. Without his leadership, it almost certainly would have failed.

No doubt there are conscious people, Marxists, who consider this a none too subtle hint that they in turn should get active and form a truly Marxist party, a Communist Party to lead the working class. My only response is that you are correct. The proletariat is doing their part, and it is up to Marxists to do their part. It may help to consider this your duty, because that is precisely what it is. Without Marxist leadership, it is very likely that the revolution will fail, be diverted by the bourgeoisie, and will merely result in a different method of rule, by the same reactionary class. There is no shortage of servants of the bourgeoisie, including those who masquerade as Marxists, who are anxious to preserve the rule of the bourgeoisie. Of course the workers are confused, which is the reason I recommend the title, Communist Party, Dictatorship of the Proletariat. It is that Dictatorship which can serve to distinguish the true revolutionary Marxist from the revisionists.

This is not to say that Sanders is a revisionist, as he most certainly is not. At no point has Sanders ever claimed to be a Marxist, but an Independent Socialist. This is to say that he is a utopian socialist, and history has proven that all previous attempts at creating a utopian society have failed. Without doubt, this current attempt, on behalf of Sanders, will also fail.

These are facts, just as it is a fact that Sanders has the support of countless working people. For that reason, we should offer Sanders our unqualified support, encouraging people to campaign for Sanders, carry banners and signs in support, join the two mainstream political parties and endorse Sanders for president. At the same time, we should make our position perfectly clear that no change of face, in Washington, will change the fact that the capitalists, the bourgeoisie, are in charge. There is one way, and only one way to overthrow the bourgeoisie and establish a socialist society, and that is through revolution and the subsequent Dictatorship of the Proletariat.

The further fact is that the working people have got to learn this from their own experience. That is the reason it is so important to support Sanders for president. It is the best way to prepare people for the revolution, to train the most advanced workers for the key positions they will have to occupy after we overthrow the bourgeoisie and establish the Dictatorship of the Proletariat.

With that in mind, I can only suggest slogans, to be placed on banners and posters:

Workers of the World, Unite!
Scientific Socialism!
Dictatorship of the Proletariat!
Sanders For President!

15

PRIMARIES AND CAUCUSES

The voting in the Nevada caucuses has just finished, and citizens who are not confused are simply not aware of what is happening. The journalists are cheerfully reporting opinion polls which contradict reality. Those same journalists are contradicting each other, and they are even contradicting themselves. Perhaps the purpose of the opinion polls is to confuse people. If that is the case, they are doing a fine job.

In the interest of clarifying the situation, we must first explain that there is a difference between primaries and caucuses. Primary elections are run by state and local governments. By contrast, caucuses are private events that are directly run by the political parties themselves. Further, primaries use secret ballots for voting. On the other hand, caucuses are local gatherings of voters who vote at the end of the meeting for a particular candidate. Then it moves to nominating conventions, during which each political party selects a candidate to endorse.

Some states use the primary election process, while other states use the caucuses process. The end result is to determine a certain number of electors for a particular candidate, based on its total number of representatives in Congress. Each elector casts one electoral vote following the general election. There are a total of 538 electoral votes. The candidate that gets more than half, which is of course 270, wins the election. That is the way Trump won the election.

The important thing to remember and to drive home to the members of the public, the working class and the middle class, is that the votes cast during the general election serve basically no purpose. *It is only after the general election that the president is elected!*

But before the general election the "powers that be" have placed the primaries and caucuses. These are being presented as an important part of the "democratic process". Even though it is something of a farce, it is important to vote, so citizens should be encouraged to cast their ballots.

The polls opened early in the state of Nevada, and the early voting was most impressive. Apparently it was a record turn out. This is an indication of the strength of the revolutionary movement, which is clearly broad and deep.

The press is reporting a shortage of volunteers at the voting booths. All candidates can afford to spend millions on campaign financing, in some cases tens and even hundreds of millions. Yet those same candidates expect workers to volunteer their time, to work at the voting booths, probably with little or no training, and do a professional job. When this does not happen, as the gong show in Iowa clearly proves, the candidates complain bitterly. Perhaps it should be suggested, to the candidates, that they should work at

the booths and show people how to do a proper job! For
that matter, I suppose it never occurred to them to pay those
people who are performing their democratic duty.

Now that Sanders has officially been declared the winner
of the Nevada caucus, the journalists are not at all happy.
They are now being forced to face the fact that the Sanders
campaign is gaining momentum. People across the country
are becoming excited about the idea of having a socialist
president. Sanders is now a force with which they have to face.

As there is a crowded field of candidates for the Democratic
presidential nomination, it is doubtful that any one candidate
will win a majority of delegates needed to win, at the
Democratic National Convention. The candidates who
wins a certain minimum amount of votes in each state will
secure a number of delegates to vote for that candidate at the
Democratic National Convention. At least, that is the best
I can gather. If no one candidate has a majority of delegates,
then a second round of voting will take place and the "Super
Delegates" will be allowed to cast their vote. No one quite
knows just how these people are selected, probably by the
party bosses. Certainly the American voters have nothing
to say in the manner. The fact remains that these Super
Delegates are quite numerous and can easily determine
the Democratic candidate for the presidency. American
democracy at its finest!

The capitalists and the party bosses within the Democratic
Party, the card carrying members of the party, are consoling
themselves with the thought of the Super Delegates throwing
the nomination to a candidate other than Sanders. The hell
with what the voters want!

No doubt the speech Sanders gave immediately after winning the Nevada caucus was cause for concern to the bourgeoisie. He promised to raise the minimum wage to 15 dollars per hour. Also more well paying union jobs, free college tuition, the cancellation of all student loans, housing for the homeless and universal health care. He also promises to challenge the pharmaceutical industry, impose a Wall Street tax, reform the criminal justice system, end private prisons, legalize marijuana, expunge the records of those convicted of possessing marijuana and reform immigration. Then there is his plan to place the country on the road to sustainable energy, away from fossil fuels. As for all the firearm violence, the mass murders, he promises universal background checks and to ban the sale of assault weapons. There will be an end to the current policy of separating babies from their mothers and placing children in jail. Bravo Bernie Sanders!

Each and every one of these promises is completely reasonable, at least from the standpoint of the common people. From the standpoint of the capitalists, the bourgeoisie, each and every one of those promises is completely unreasonable, absolutely out of the question.

This is all the more reason to support Sanders for president. It is clear that the American people have spontaneously gravitated to the Left, towards socialism. That is fine, as far as it goes. Now it is up to conscious people, Marxists, to explain to them that the capitalists will never allow a peaceful transition to socialism. They will do whatever it takes to stop Sanders. In the process, the working people will learn that we are right. The experience will not be a pleasant one. There is simply no other way.

The best way we can support Sanders is by having Americans join the two mainstream political parties. As card carrying members of the parties, they can nominate Sanders for president, as both Democrat and Republican. They can also nominate numerous other Leftist people for offices, on a state and federal level. As well, they can amend the Constitution, by a vote of two thirds of the states, to abolish the Electoral College. There is also the not so little matter of carrying signs and posters which put forward our belief in revolution and scientific socialism. Last but not least, it is absolutely necessary to form a true Marxist Communist Party, separate from our support for Sanders.

It is to be hoped that women and students, those who have proven themselves to be such excellent organizers, will once again come together, as they did at the time of the swearing in of Trump, and get behind Sanders. We want that support to be as broad based as possible. With that in mind, it is further hoped that people will put aside their differences and come together for a common cause.

By contrast, the true Communist Party must be supremely exclusive, composed only of true Marxists, those who endorse the Dictatorship of the Proletariat. The goal of the Party is to raise the level of awareness of the working class, to prepare them for the revolution and subsequent socialism, in the form of the Dictatorship of the Proletariat. The most advanced workers will have to be raised to the level of Marxists, true conscious people.

Time is not on our side, as the revolution could break out at any time. As people are now enthusiastic about Sanders, the capitalists may provoke a revolution very soon.

With that in mind, feel free to educate the public with Marxist slogans:

Workers of the World, Unite!
Scientific Socialism!
Dictatorship of the Proletariat!
Sanders For President!

16

SOUTH CAROLINA AND SUPER TUESDAY

The farce of determining a candidate for the presidency of the United States, on behalf of the Democratic Party, is now proceeding to the fourth state of South Carolina. Immediately after that, comes the major "jackpot" of Super Tuesday, in which eleven states will get to decide the number of delegates to assign to different candidates. The two big prizes are the states of California and Texas. The press is focused on this "election" to the exclusion of almost everything else.

For that reason, no doubt most members of the working class are also paying attention, if for no other reason than that they watch the news. As that is the case, Marxists should also be paying close attention. The only way to raise the level of awareness of the working class is by taking an interest in that which interests the working class, and using these as particulars in order to drive home the general, which is the fact that classes exist. Further, workers are members of a class of people called the proletariat, and the billionaires are members of a class of people called the bourgeoisie. The bourgeoisie is the ruling class, one which crushes and exploits the working class. The bourgeoisie must be overthrown and this can only be done through revolution. It is these points which must be driven home to the working class.

Among the numerous candidates, the only self described Independent Socialist is Bernie Sanders, and he clearly has the support of countless people. The press reports that the "establishment" is worried, determined to stop Sanders. As Sanders is so popular, there is now a "sense of panic" within the Democratic Party. Among his rivals for the candidacy, Buttigieg is reported to be accusing Sanders of having an "inflexible ideological revolution that leaves out most Democrats, not to mention most Americans", one which "defies conventional wisdom". Anyone who "defies conventional wisdom" is a person to be admired, so the intended insult is in reality a compliment.

The press is reporting that the "establishment" is in a panic, concerned that the public loves Sanders and his "momentum is building". They are concerned that the young people support Sanders, and the "moderates" are moving to the "left" in support. They are afraid that if Sanders does well in South Carolina and on Super Tuesday, then he is sure to be "unstoppable", which is to say that he will be the candidate for president, on behalf on the Democratic Party. The press further reports that even Trump is worried, as well he should be.

Numerous progressive people, including politicians and celebrities, are now endorsing Sanders. These include Michael Moore, a fine film maker and a thorn in the side of the capitalists, the bourgeoisie. As well, Alexandria Ocasio-Cortez, AOC, a member of Congress and a leader of the working class, has referred to the growing support of Sanders as "a mass movement of working class people… multi racial, multi gendered, multi generational". In this, she is absolutely correct.

It is encouraging that the press and the candidates are now using the word "class", even if is being used incorrectly. Since the creation of the country, it has been customary to deny the existence of classes, at least in America. Now they are indirectly acknowledging that such things as classes exist, so that they are moving closer to the truth. They still confuse the issue by claiming that those of us who work for a living are middle class, rather than being working class, proletarians. Then too, the super rich are referred to as the "billionaire class". As yet, they continue to avoid the correct term, bourgeoisie.

In fact, the billionaires are a member of a class of people referred to as the bourgeoisie, and they are completely reactionary. That leaves the middle class, the petty bourgeois. There are still a few small business owners, although the bourgeoisie, through their control of monopolies, are driving ever more members of the middle class into bankruptcy. That leaves the peasants, or farmers, and the family farm is going the way of the small business owner, which is precisely what it is. A family farm is a small business. As the monopolies become ever stronger, ever more complete, no competition is tolerated.

It is notable that Marxists have been quite silent during this whole "election process". Perhaps they think that the Electoral College is archaic, a relic of the days of slavery. So it is, and must be abolished, but for the moment, it has the attention of the working people. As that is the case, it must be used to raise the level of awareness of the proletariat.

The fact is that Sanders, as well as the press, has been doing a fine job of documenting the lies and hypocrisy of Trump. This is not high praise, as Trump is the poster child for hypocrisy. Any school child could point out the fact that he lies constantly. Some people speculate that he was born that way, but it is more likely something he learned, growing up as a member of the bourgeoisie. It is safe to say that all members of the bourgeoisie are liars. Trump is merely the most visible presence.

No doubt the bourgeoisie are puzzled by Sanders. As they are a pack of thieves and liars, and expect nothing less from all others, to confront an honest man is a novel experience. They are truly bewildered, determined to stop him, but unsure of how to proceed.

The support of Sanders is growing, even extending to those who were formerly considered to be "right wing". This includes members of the Republican Party, even current and former members of the Trump administration. They are increasingly becoming disillusioned, seeking an alternative. The idea of abandoning their beloved Republican Party would likely never occur to them, and such people tend to be rabidly anti union. But then they may be open to the idea of an "association", which is merely a union with a different spelling.

Contrary to popular belief, Trump is not splitting the country apart. The country has always been split apart. The proletariat, the working class, has always been at war with the bourgeoisie, a "cold war", even though most workers were not aware of this. Now that the working class is in motion, the war is now more open, about to break out into open conflict, a "hot war", to borrow an expression from the bourgeoisie. Trump is merely forcing people to openly choose a side. So be it.

For that reason, I am suggesting that people, those who were formerly middle class, set up an association, or a society, which is non partisan. It must be as broad based as possible, open to as many people as possible. As Lenin phrased it, the task of Communists is "to *convince* the backward elements, to work *among* them, and not to *fence themselves* off from them." (italics by Lenin) The purpose of the society can be to strive towards a democratic republic, for example. For that matter, people with common interests can band together for a common goal. Such societies may not support the revolutionary motion, but very likely will not oppose it either. We may think of this as being in a position of "benevolent neutrality".

I am also suggesting that all Americans join the two parties, as card carrying members, party bosses, thus being able to influence party policy. They can also determine the candidates for any and all political offices. It is only natural that people should want to be part of something greater than themselves. After all, we are all herd animals, although we prefer to think of that as just being sociable. At the same time, those who have been cursed with the bourgeois ideology are determined to "get ahead". Such an outlook is particularly characteristic of professional people. We have to respect the fact that they are prejudiced against unions, while at the same time offering them the comfort and security of an organization greater than themselves.

A great many people, including those who have never been accused of having any "Leftist" beliefs, are convinced that there is a "ground swell" of support for Sanders. They fully expect this to grow and strengthen. It will very likely spread across the country, unless it already has, and Sanders will very likely be the Democratic Party candidate for president. It is further thought that in such a case, Sanders is sure to be the next president. Most people find this rather exciting. The strongest supporters of Trump and the bourgeoisie are the most excited. In fact, they are frantically trying to find some way to stop Sanders.

Those of us who are Marxists are well aware that the bourgeoisie are in charge and fully intend to remain in charge. They are not about to give up their power and wealth without a fight. They are not about to allow a socialist, even an Independent Socialist, to become president. This is all the more reason to support Sanders and many other Leftist people who would like to run for office. No doubt the bourgeoisie will make every effort to crush any and all such efforts. It may help to think of this as an educational opportunity, a school for socialists, provided by the bourgeoisie.

Our goal is not to establish a socialist society through the democratic process, because this cannot be done. The bourgeoisie will never allow this. Our goal is to raise the level of awareness of the proletariat to the level of Marxists, and this can be done only by becoming involved in the struggles of the proletariat. At the moment, that means the Democratic primaries. It is our duty to support them, while at the same time making clear our position that the bourgeoisie has to be overthrown, the state apparatus has to be crushed and a new state apparatus has to be set up, in order to crush the bourgeoisie under the Dictatorship of the Proletariat.

With that in mind, I can suggest the posters and banners call for our usual revolutionary slogans as well as support for Sanders:

Sanders For President!
Abolish the Electoral College!
Join the Two Parties!
Workers of the World, Unite!
Scientific Socialism!
Dictatorship of the Proletariat!

17

SANDERS AND THE ELECTORAL COLLEGE

As I write this, the voting in South Carolina to determine the presidential candidate of the Democratic Party is under way. It is an understatement to say the Democratic Party bosses are worried. It is more accurate to say that those same bosses are nearly in panic mode. They are terrified that Senator Sanders will win enough electoral votes to clinch the nomination of the Democratic Party, in order to run for president. As there is an upsurge in revolutionary motion to the Left, in that a great many Americans are spontaneously gravitating towards socialism, there is good reason for their concern.

Now is the time for conscious people, Marxists, to take advantage of this spontaneous movement of the members of the public, in order to raise their level of awareness. We have got to transform this vague fondness of socialism into a love of scientific socialism, and not just utopian socialism. As an explanation, we should add that Sanders is a self described Independent Socialist, which is to say a utopian socialist, not a Marxist, a scientific socialist.

The best way to prove to the members of the public that utopian socialism does not work is by endorsing a socialist for president, in this case Sanders. Further, it is also correct to endorse candidates for other offices, who refer to themselves as socialists or just plain Leftist people. The idea is to flood Washington and all state capitals with Leftist people.

As for the skeptics who consider this to be no more than a "pipe dream", may I suggest that all Americans join the two mainstream political parties, Democratic and Republican, as card carrying members, referred to as party bosses. Those same party bosses can then determine the candidate to run for any and all political office. As long as the same candidate is running for office on behalf of both parties, the campaign expenses should be kept to a minimum. In that case, there will be no need to ask for campaign contributions, thereby also keeping the influence of capital to a minimum. As a bonus, those same candidates, once elected, can determine, by an act of Congress or two thirds of the states, to amend the Constitution and abolish the Electoral College.

It is not only the party bosses who are determined to stop Sanders. The other presidential contenders are also focused on Sanders. It is best to bear in mind that each of the candidates is well coached. The millions they receive in campaign contributions is spent on something more than television ads. They also spend a small fortune on "handlers", as is the common expression. These include professional make up artists, wardrobe experts, hair stylists, speech writers, "body language" experts, which is to say those who train candidates on proper tone of voice, posture, gestures and the correct response to anticipated questions. The presidential contenders who give the best impression are those who have managed to hire the finest coaches.

This was illustrated quite clearly in a recent "town hall". Senator Elizabeth Warren was asked by a citizen: "Can you explain why the will of the voters should not matter if no candidate reaches a majority of delegates?" -Way to go, citizen!- It is possible the citizen was told to ask that question, or not. Either way, Warren was prepared for the answer. She immediately "pivoted" and said that in the last federal election, Sanders also felt that way.

Clearly, Warren had a fine coach. She was trained to turn the question onto Sanders, otherwise known as pivoting, and avoided a direct answer.

An even more illuminating answer was given by the Speaker of the House, Nancy Pelosi. For the purpose of this article, I refer to the House of Representatives as the Congress, which is the name most people use. Her response, to a question concerning Sanders, was quite instructive: "It is not unusual for a party platform or the candidates for president to have their own aggenda that they would put forth. And it is not unusual for the House of Representatives to have its aggenda, as well. We have to win in certain particular areas. We are not about a popular vote in the country or in particular states, in terms of your Electoral College. We are in district by district. And thats how we won last time we demonstrated that we know how to win." To say that this she makes no sense, is an understatement.

This little speech was given by one of the most powerful people in Washington, and one of the finest members of the "establishment". As she is the Speaker of the House, Nancy Pelosi is the person who runs the Congress. Further, as the Congress controls the money, it is safe to say that she is arguably the most powerful person in Washington. She is certainly one of the most intelligent. Yet this same speech makes clear that even Nancy Pelosi, the best of the lot, has been reduced to muddled thinking. As Lenin put it, they "cannot help committing irreparable blunders. That, in fact, is what will bring about the downfall of the bourgeoise."

He went on to explain that as we are all human, we all make mistakes. The difference is that the mistakes we make, as Marxists, tend to be minor and easily rectified. Such mistakes can only be rectified by first acknowledging that we made a mistake. The bourgeoisie are not capable of admitting that they made a mistake, regardless of the magnitude of that mistake, and are therefore not capable of rectifying that mistake.

To return to the question the citizen asked, it is entirely possible that Sanders endorsed the Electoral College four years ago. That is of no concern to us. We are endorsing Sanders because he says he is a socialist. The fact that the citizen wants to abolish the Electoral College -otherwise the question makes no sense- implies that there are a great many Americans who feel the same way. All such Americans should be encouraged to join the two parties and amend the Constitution.

As we are still cursed with the Electoral College, perhaps it is best to do the math. It is reported that there are 3,979 delegates, so that a candidate needs 1,991 delegates in order to win the nomination. It is also reported that of the 3,979 delegates, 3,208 are "pledged" delegates, and by law, have to vote the way their voters told them. The remaining 771 are Super Delegates. These Super Delegates are independent, not pledged delegates, but "party leaders and elected officials". If, in the first round of voting, no one candidate wins a majority, then in the second round of voting, the Super Delegates can vote and very likely determine the candidate to run for president, on behalf of the Democratic Party.

No wonder the citizen is concerned! This is the political system that the leaders of the Democratic Party want to maintain, along with all the candidates except Sanders. Way to go, Sanders!

In order to preserve their method of rule, the monopoly capitalists, the bourgeoisie, have determined to enter a small army of candidates into the primaries. In this way, they are attempting to "split the vote", so that there is no chance that Sanders will secure a majority of electoral votes on the first round of voting, at the Democratic National Convention. That will force a second round of votes, giving the Super Delegates the opportunity to secure the nomination of a candidate whom is acceptable to the bourgeoisie. Or so they hope.

The success -or failure- of this plan depends largely upon the strength of the revolutionary motion. That is where the Marxists come in. The working class needs leaders, but that is not to say that the leaders of the proletariat must be proletarians. Anyone who says otherwise is a demagogue. The only proper leaders of the working class are those who are aware of the scientific, revolutionary theories of Marx and

Lenin. Whether those leaders are working class or middle class, is of no consequence.

This brings us to the primary in South Carolina. The journalists are reporting that it is a "must win" state for Biden, the former Vice President. As I write this, it has just been reported that "Biden won big". No doubt the capitalists are breathing a sigh of relief.

Now all eyes are focused on the primaries on Super Tuesday. It is reported that perhaps as many as a third of the delegates are up for grabs. As Marxists, our only concern is in raising the level of awareness of the proletariat. We are not "election watchers". It is disappointing that the press is reporting no demonstrations or marches. May I suggest that the various Leftist groups across the country come together, put aside your differences and focus on a common enemy. That common enemy is not Trump. It is the bourgeoisie. They can and must be crushed, and that will happen only through revolution and the subsequent Dictatorship of the Proletariat. Now it is a matter of making the proletariat aware of this.

With that in mind, I will end this article with my usual slogans:

Sanders For President!
Unite the Left!
Scientific Socialism!
Workers of the World, Unite!

18

SANDERS, SUPER TUESDAY AND THE CORONA VIRUS

Now that the South Carolina primary is behind us, the press is focused on "Super Tuesday". As the working people watch the news, and in fact they pay strict attention to the news, it is up to conscious people, Marxists, to also watch the news. The only way in which we can hope to raise the level of awareness of the proletariat and bring that awareness to the level of Marxists, is by becoming involved in that which interests the workers. At the moment, that is the Democratic primaries, and in particular the nomination of the self declared independent socialist, Bernie Sanders. The corona virus is also in the news.

The press is most generously assisting us in our noble endeavour, although they, no doubt, are not aware of this. They are quite cheerfully pointing out the fact that in the "Nordic" countries, which are thought to be socialist, there are more billionaires, per capita, than there are in America. These facts are carefully documented, as is the fact that the highest taxes are paid by the "middle class and poor people".

Note that they are careful not to use the correct scientific expressions of petty bourgeois and proletarians, and of course the bourgeoisie are referred to as billionaires. This is consistent with the North American lie, as propagated by the American bourgeoisie, that classes do not exist.

Those of us who are scientific socialists, which is to say Marxists, have been saying right along that utopian socialism does not work. Sanders has his own version of utopian socialism, which he refers to as "independent socialism". This is merely a "rose by a different name", a different shade of the same colour. The only effective socialism is scientific socialism, as expressed by Marx, and that is in the form of the Dictatorship of the Proletariat. That is the one and only way in which the class enemies of the proletariat, the bourgeoisie, can be crushed, after they are overthrown through revolution.

It is only the proletariat that can emancipate the proletariat. No amount of well meaning middle class utopian socialists can do this for the working class. Further, in a monopoly capitalist country such as America, one which has so fervently embraced imperialism, there can be no thought of a peaceful transition to socialism. The one and only way in which socialism can be established is through violent revolution. That revolution could break out any day now.

The country can be compared to a "powder keg", in that any spark could set off an explosion. It is entirely possible that the other item in the news, that of the "corona virus", could well be that spark. We have no way of knowing. We do know that the stock markets have been tumbling, and may continue to tumble. We also know that Trump is speaking of a "miracle", in that the corona virus will magically disappear, while his son, Donald Trump, Junior, is saying that the Democrats are hoping that "millions of people will die from this sickness, just to make President Trump look bad".

It is characteristic of the bourgeoisie that a sickness which is killing thousands, concerns them only in so far as it affects their wealth and power. People are dying and they are concerned because it is affecting the stock market! It is facts such as these which should be driven home to the working class.

As working people are paying attention to the press reports concerning the stock market, feel free to explain that the capitalists refer to a drop of ten percent as a "correction", while a drop of twenty percent they refer to as a "bear market". Then there is a recession and the dreaded "D word", a depression. As yet, they have not dared to use that word. If, as medical experts fear, this virus spreads around the world and becomes a pandemic, then they may be forced to use that word. A depression could be "right around the corner".

Explain to the working people that the capitalists have tied together the economies of the world. That which has an effect on the economy of one country affects the economies of all countries. As the journalists are quick to point out, the fear of becoming infected with the virus causes people to avoid travel, and the profits of airlines and ocean cruise vessels, among others, takes a "nose dive". Then too, as people cannot go to work, for fear of catching the virus, factories shut down. The companies which count upon the goods provided by these factories are also affected. As China is most effected by the virus, and because so many companies now buy from China, the "ripple effect" is felt throughout the world. So say the journalists, and they are probably correct, as far as they go.

No doubt the workers are aware of recessions and depressions. The more advanced workers may ask the difference between the two. The capitalists have a definition, which may not be very accurate, but gives a place to start: "A recession is the contraction phase of the business cycle. A common rule of thumb for recessions is two quarters of negative GDP growth. A depression is a prolonged period of economic recession, marked by a significant decline in income and employment. There is no widely accepted definition of depressions". We may add that GDP stands for Gross Domestic Product, while a quarter is a three month period.

That is the best definition the capitalists can provide, for what it is worth. Those same capitalists are blaming the drop in the stock market on the corona virus. Although that may be a contributing factor, that is far from the whole story.

A more accurate explanation is provided by Lenin, in his book, Imperialism, the Highest Stage of Capitalism. As he phrases it, "The statement that cartels can abolish crises is a fable spread by bourgeois economists whom at all cost desire to place capitalism in a favourable light. On the contrary, when monopoly appears in *certain* branches of industry, it increases and intensifies the anarchy inherent in capitalist production *as a whole*." We may add that by now, monopoly has taken root in almost all branches of industry.

It is clear that the corona virus is not responsible for the "correction" in the stock market, just it will not be responsible for any possible "bear market", never mind recession or depression. These crisis in capitalism are a natural result of that which Lenin explains as "the extremely rapid rate of technical progress gives rise more and more to disturbances in the coordination between the various spheres of industry, to anarchy and crisis." Lenin goes on to say that "Crises of every kind-economic crises more frequently, *but not only these*- in their turn increase considerably the tendency towards concentration and monopoly". Perhaps the key statement is "economic crises more frequently, but not only these". (my italics) It is entirely possible that we may be facing an economic crisis along with a medical crisis, that which the capitalists may refer to as a "perfect storm".

The capitalists are referring to a possible "panic" among politicians, those who are terrified at the prospect of Sanders becoming the Democratic Party nominee for president. They are also reporting "panic" among stock brokers. Perhaps a bit of this "panic", or at least deep concern, should extend to the Left. We have no way of knowing what will happen to the stock market, just as we cannot predict the course of the outbreak of the corona virus. We do not expect a "miracle", as Trump suggested. We do know that the revolutionary motion is becoming more intense and could explode any day now. We also know that an economic crisis, such as a severe downturn in the stock market, could rapidly intensify the conflict. As could a rapid spread in the virus. The two together could lead to a complete out break of hostilities, revolutionary war.

I mention this as an incentive to all Leftist people. Feel free to come together and take action. Put aside your differences, at least until after the revolution. For that matter, by the time the revolution is over, your differences may be pointless. The revolution may resolve those differences. But in the mean time, join the two mainstream political parties. Run for office. Encourage your families and friends to do the same. Organize protests and demonstrations. Disrupt the town halls and primaries the capitalists so love. Women and students have worked miracle before, now do it again. Only this time carry the protests through to the revolution. Do not rest until the bourgeoisie are overthrown and crushed under the Dictatorship of the Proletariat. Last but not least, Marxists must come together and form a Communist Party, Dictatorship of the Proletariat. For the Love of God, take action!

The revolution will not wait until you are ready. The proletariat is counting on you.

I most fervently hope and pray that many members of the working class, those who are just now becoming politically active- Welcome, my Brothers and Sisters, my Comrades!- are reading this article. With that in mind, I can only point out that the best way to get the attention of as many people as possible is with slogans. It is a place to start. Feel free to come up with slogans of your choice, but these are suggestions only:

Unite the Left!
Join the two Parties!
Sanders For President!
Scientific Socialism!
Workers of the World, Unite!

19

SUPER TUESDAY AND THE ELECTORAL COLLEGE

The Nevada primary is now history, and the small herd of Democratic candidates for the nomination for the presidency has thinned out slightly. Steyer has just thrown in the towel, so that is one less member of the bourgeoisie who wants to occupy the oval office, while another billionaire, Bloomberg, has yet to run in even one primary. That has not stopped him from already spending a reported *400 million dollars* on his candidacy. Altogether, he and the other candidates have spent a *billion dollars*, and there is still eight months to go before the election!

Perhaps the Leftist people should disrupt these "town halls" and "primary debates" with signs and posters which question the wisdom of spending such money on advertising, when there are so many people who are homeless, hungry, working for minimum wage or unemployed, scraping by as best they can on food stamps. The bourgeoise can afford to waste such money on campaigns, but have no money for the working class.

As I write this, I have just learned of a "town hall" meeting which was disrupted and even cancelled in Minnesota, the home state of Senator Amy Klobuchar. She was not allowed to speak, forced to leave the high school, due to the protests of Black Lives Matter. This is certainly encouraging, and we hope to see more such disruptions. It is hoped that further disruptions of such meetings will contain class content, going beyond the racial implications. Possibly as a result of this -it could be that Klobuchar can take a hint- she has just thrown in the towel, will no longer attempt to run for the presidency. It may have occurred to her that as she cannot campaign even in her home state, the reception she is bound to receive in other states is bound to be even more discouraging.

Or it could be that the bourgeoisie, working through their loyal boot licking servants, have decided that the best way to stop Sanders is by narrowing down the field. They may have ordered Klobuchar to step aside, while at the same time ordering her to throw her support behind the former Vice President, Biden. The same could well be true of Pete Buttigieg, a candidate who has also stepped aside and endorsed Biden.

The latest line of political hog wash is that the Democratic Party has to appeal to the "moderate" wing of the Democratic Party. Apparently those who have rather spontaneously gravitated towards socialism are considered to be too "radical". Very soon, those who consider utopian socialism to be radical will be faced with scientific socialism, in the form of the Dictatorship of the Proletariat. Then they will learn the meaning of the word radical, at least in the form of the Dictatorship.

The press is further reporting that the field is narrowing down to Sanders versus Biden. As it is common practice for government officials to "leak" classified information to the press, it is reasonable to assume that they have access to plans and details which the capitalists would prefer to conceal from the public. But then the capitalists are also constantly squabbling among themselves. As a means of "stabbing the other in the back", one will disclose confidential information to the press, "off the record", which is bourgeois speak for preferring to remain anonymous. As the members of the press have the democratic right, as guaranteed in the Constitution, to refuse to reveal their sources, this is perfectly legal.

Now the press is focusing on Biden versus Sanders, or capitalism versus socialism, although as yet they are careful to avoid the word capitalism. They are using the expression "results versus revolution", which is not terribly accurate but a step in the right direction. Not that Sanders is a revolutionary, and is not calling for revolution, but the bourgeoisie are thoughtfully raising the issue. As their thinking is now completely muddled, this is not too surprising.

Sanders has responded to this attack by saying that the government supports and gives tax breaks to the sixty billionaires in the country. Someone should correct him, in that there are over ten times that many billionaires in the country. Aside from that little detail, he is absolutely correct.

It is up to conscious people, by whom I of course mean Marxists, to point out that the "results" to which Biden is referring, is nothing other than reforms. As a utopian socialist, Sanders is of course determined to "change the system from within", which means no revolution. He refers to himself as an "Independent Socialist", which is another term for a utopian socialist, and such misguided souls actually believe it is possible to elect Leftist people to any and all political office, including the presidency, and establish a socialist, democratic republic, under capitalism. These are their beliefs, and we have got to respect those beliefs, especially as a great many common people are also of that opinion.

It is further the duty of Marxists *-wake up, people!-* to assist Sanders and other Leftist people, whether socialist, democratic, communist, Marxist or just plain working class progressive, to run for any and all political office. This will serve the dual purpose of raising their level of awareness, as well as the awareness of the working class, and provide valuable training for the Dictatorship of the Proletariat. After the revolution, workers will, of necessity, be placed in key positions of authority. Any training they receive now, under capitalism, will prove to be most valuable.

That is the reason I am suggesting that all Americans join the two mainstream political parties, as card carrying members, party bosses. I have no doubt the students and seniors, in particular, will be anxious to do so. Then, as party bosses, they can nominate their own candidates for all offices, on behalf of both parties. Once elected, those politicians can fight for free tuition, cancellation of all student loans, free medical, increase the pensions, raise the minimum wage, housing for the homeless, guaranteed annual income, welcome to immigrants, etc. This can all be paid for by forcing the billionaires, the bourgeoisie, to pay their fair share of taxes. As if that is about to happen!

As all Marxists are well aware, the bourgeoisie are in charge and fully intend to remain in charge. No change of face in Washington or anywhere else is about to change that. At the point where their authority is challenged, when "push comes to shove", then they will change their method of rule. That point is rapidly approaching.

For what it is worth, this infatuation with reforms is characteristic of all utopian socialists, as well as all "would be" Marxists. Those who claim to be Marxists, but are focused only on reforms, denying the necessity for revolution and the Dictatorship of the Proletariat, are referred to as revisionists. Some of these people openly admit the fact that they believe Marxism should be revised, while others deny this, while practicing it in deeds. Either way, the fact of the matter is that any reforms they manage to secure, under capitalism, are absolutely paltry.

Also in the news, the Republicans are concerned that Biden may be a threat, so they are trying to open a "Burisma Probe", in an attempt to discredit the former Vice President. The fact that he very likely had nothing to do with any illegal activity which may or may not have taken place, is of no consequence. They are also reported to be "deposing" Hillary Clinton, over her role in the "email scandal", whatever that is. The idea is to "throw mud" at the democrats, as that is the popular expression.

As working people watch the news, and in fact they follow the news rather closely, it is up to Marxists to also pay close attention to that which is being reported. We can then use these news items as a means of raising the level of awareness of the working class. From the point of view of the capitalists, the significance of "Super Tuesday" lies in the fact that fourteen states have primaries on that day, with a third of the delegates "up for grabs". From the point of view of Marxists, the significance lies strictly in the fact that it makes a mockery of the democratic process. It is strictly democracy for the bourgeoisie. The abolition of the Electoral College can only serve to make their rule more difficult. Now that is a cause which should serve to unite all Leftist people!

As I write this, the results of the Super Tuesday votes are being reported, and the capitalists are delighted that Biden is a clear front runner. He now has more delegates who are committed to him than Sanders. That concerns us, as Marxists, because that concerns working people. It is also being reported, by self described political "pundits", that the allocation of delegates is quite complicated. It depends not only on the state, but also on the district within the state, and the rules change according to the will of the leaders of the Democratic Party. The only reason they have for mentioning this is because their viewers, the members of the public, the working people, are trying to make sense of this.

It is not the duty of Marxists to explain to working people the precise details of the electoral system, especially as the party bosses change those rules, as they see fit, in order to maintain the rule of the capitalists, the bourgeoisie. It is sufficient to choose one detail, such as the role of "Super Delegates", those who are not elected, but chosen by the party bosses, and vote as the bosses order. From the particular, it is necessary to go to the general, which is the fact that Trump is not the problem. The problem is the fact that the bourgeoisie rule, and will continue to rule, until they are overthrown and crushed under the Dictatorship of the Proletariat.

The fact is that conscious people, Marxists, tend to be former or current members of the middle class, the petty bourgeois. The reason is that members of the working class tend to be not terribly well educated, through no fault of their own. The bourgeoisie goes to great length to make sure of this. That in no way changes the fact that workers, or at least the most advanced members of the proletariat, must be raised to the level of Marxist. They will lead, and the less advanced will follow.

The best way to raise the level of awareness of the workers -if not the only way- is by becoming involved in matters which interest them. At the moment, that means the primaries and the approaching presidential election. It is reported that the primaries will run until possibly June, although the party bosses can change this, as they see fit. That in no way changes the fact that this has the attention of the public, the working class and the middle class, so it is up to Marxists to *get active!*

Explain to working people, in terms they can understand, the fact that they are members of a class of people referred to as the proletariat, and that the monopoly capitalists, the billionaires, are members of a class of people referred to as the bourgeoisie. Further, our interests are diametrically opposed. Be sure to use popular language followed by scientific terms, as workers have to learn these terms. At the same time, do not be condescending.

Encourage people to join the two mainstream political parties, as card carrying members, party bosses. Also encourage more marches, more disruptions of town halls, rallies and primaries. Make every effort to unite the Left. Carry banners and posters which contain class content. Support Sanders for president, as well as Leftist candidates for other offices. Harass the bourgeoisie at all opportunities. Allow them no peace.

In the interests of raising the level of awareness of as many people as possible, the use of slogans is recommended. It gives people a place to start. With that in mind, may I suggest:

Sanders For President!
Abolish the Electoral College!
Unite the Left!
Scientific Socialism!
Workers of the World, Unite!
Dictatorship of the Proletariat!

20

MARCH 10 PRIMARIES, SUPER TUESDAY 2

Now that Super Tuesday is a thing of the past, the journalists are in their glory. They are quite cheerfully reporting that Biden is the clear front runner, and it appears to be a two way race between Biden and Sanders. The billionaire who dropped out, Mike Bloomberg, is now supporting Biden. As Bloomberg has already spent *half* a *billion* of his own money, he has a "party machine" well established. He is reported to have hundreds, if not thousands of people, serving at his beck and call. He and numerous other politicians have bent over backwards, in an effort to show their support for Biden.

The reason I mention this is because it is the very thing the common people are watching, if for no other reason than they have no choice in the matter. Working people watch the news and discuss it, in an attempt to make sense of that which is happening. It is up to conscious people, Marxists, to explain to working people, in terms which they can understand, precisely what is happening. It is the duty of the journalists to sanitize the news, to report events devoid of all class content. This they do supremely well, if only because they are not able to examine a situation in class terms.

The significance of the fact that Bloomberg has enlisted a small army of people to work in the political arena is an example of the "state apparatus" which has been set up by the capitalists, the bourgeoisie, as a means of crushing the working class, the proletariat. This is the point which must be driven home to the working people, using common terms followed by the correct scientific terms, at least for the benefit of the most advanced. More popular terms can be used for the less advanced, while being careful not to be condescending.

Now we are faced with "Super Tuesday, Round Two", of March 10, in which voters of six "key states" will get to cast their ballots. In certain states, all voters are allowed to vote in the Democratic primaries, while in other states, only "registered members" of the Democratic Party are supposed to vote. In such states, those who are registered as Republicans or Independents are barred from voting in the Democratic primaries. As Donald Trump is not a complete idiot, he has noticed that such a rule is impossible to enforce. So he got the bright idea of encouraging everyone to vote in the Democratic primaries, in an attempt to disrupt the democratic process.

I think this is a fine idea, but for different reasons. It is important to encourage people to become as politically active as possible, and that certainly includes voting, wherever and whenever possible. The fact that certain voters, in certain states, may not be "allowed" to vote in the Democratic primary, yet do so anyway, may mean that those voters are being a bit "naughty". It also means that those same people are concerned with the current state of affairs, to the point where they are prepared to wait in line, in some cases for hours, for an opportunity to cast their ballot. That is most commendable, not to be discouraged. The implication is that these same voters are among the most advanced members of the public, the working class. They are doing their part, going to great length to change the system. It is safe to say that they are working to their full capacity.

Now it is up to conscious people, Marxists, to do our part. It is up to Marxists to "expand their horizons", so to speak. It is not reasonable to expect these advanced workers to take the next step, to consciously become revolutionary, to call for the overthrow of the monopoly capitalists, the bourgeoisie, and to establish the Dictatorship of the Proletariat, as *they are not aware of themselves as a class!*

Granted, there are several organizations and parties in North America who claim to be socialist, democratic socialist, independent socialist, Communist or Marxist-Leninist. Those who claim to be socialist, but not Marxist, are utopian socialists, and they deserve our respect. We are all entitled to our beliefs and we must respect the beliefs of others. This does not mean that we must share the beliefs of others. We can disagree without becoming confrontational.

This stands in sharp contrast to the people who claim to be Communist or Marxist-Leninist, but whom have revised the theories of Marx and Lenin. Some of these people openly admit to being revisionists, and for this we give them credit. They maintain that there is no need for revolution and the subsequent Dictatorship of the Proletariat, that which I consider to be the very heart and soul, the "touchstone", of Marxism. Numerous others are more subtle. They do not deny the necessity of the Dictatorship of the Proletariat, just as they do not admit this necessity. They merely avoid the issue. They are careful to make no mention of the Dictatorship of the Proletariat! This is commonly referred to as "straddling the fence", and as wits have pointed out, "must be hard on the rear end". In scientific jargon, this is referred to as "moving to the centre". In fact, it is another form of the revision of Marxism.

As it is absolutely necessary to raise the level of awareness of the working class, the proletariat, to make them aware of themselves as a class, this must be explained to them. It is hoped that by using popular terms, followed by the correct scientific terms, they will be better able to understand this. Bear in mind that the most advanced members of the proletariat must be raised to the level of awareness of Marxists.

As working people are focused on the Democratic primaries, it is up to Marxists to point out the fact that the election is "rigged", to put it in popular terms. The ability of either candidate to win a majority of delegates, at the Democratic National Convention -preferably Sanders- is determined by the party bosses. It is such people, the card carrying members of the Democratic Party, the "party bosses", who "call the shots". They make the rules and change the rules as they see fit. This is all the more reason for working people, in fact all members of the public, whether working class or middle class, to become card carrying members of both mainstream political parties, Republican and Democratic, or at least Democratic. Under no circumstances should working people be placed under any pressure to join both parties. Merely point out to people that it costs nothing, and as "party bosses", they get to determine the candidate for any and all political office. In addition, such card carrying members can make sure that the election at the Democratic National Convention is fair and "above board". For that matter, those same card carrying members, with their new political power, can take steps to amend the Constitution, abolishing the Electoral College, thus making the democratic process more democratic. Or to phrase it more accurately, they can try.

The fact of the matter is that the monopoly capitalists, the bourgeoisie, are in charge, and fully intend to remain in charge. They are not about to allow a self described "independent socialist" to separate them from their wealth and power. For that matter, Washington can be flooded with Leftist people, not that it will do any good. At least, they have every intention of making sure it does no good.

In our opinion, that of Marxists, this will do a world of good. It is sure to provide working people with valuable training towards the Dictatorship of the Proletariat. They will learn, from their own bitter experience, that the bourgeoisie are in charge and fully intend to remain in charge. After the revolution, workers with very little training, or even no training whatsoever, will be placed in positions of authority. Any training they receive now will prove most valuable after the revolution.

As there are so many self proclaimed socialists, and even self proclaimed Marxists, who deny the importance, or at best evade the issue of, the Dictatorship of the Proletariat, perhaps we had best examine the matter. Two and a half years after the Russian revolution, Lenin spoke from that experience: "The Dictatorship of the Proletariat means a most determined and most ruthless war waged by the new class against a *more powerful* enemy, the bourgeoisie, whose resistance is increased *tenfold* by their overthrow...and whose power lies, not only in the strength of international capital, the strength and durability of their international connections, but also in the *force of habit*, in the strength of *small scale production* …and small scale production *engenders* capitalism and the bourgeoisie continuously, daily, hourly, spontaneously, and on a mass scale. All these reasons make the Dictatorship of the Proletariat necessary…"(italics by Lenin)

Here in North America, thanks to the monumental efforts of the bourgeoisie to eliminate any and all competition, regardless of how insignificant that competition may be, we have far less "small scale production", but we do have a great deal of "force of habit", as well as "the strength of international capital". There are still a significant number of people, either current or former members of the middle class, the petty bourgeois, as well as many members of the working class, the proletariat, who have apparently not "received the memo", in that they are still determined to "get ahead". This is not about to happen, the "good old days" of the "little guy" owning a small business is a thing of the past. Any starry eyed optimist who dares to attempt such a thing will quickly receive his "comeuppance". In other words, the bourgeoisie will "nip such an attempt in the bud." They are not about to tolerate such "shenanigans".

As for the reader who objects to such popular language, I can only respond that I am mainly focused on the advanced members of the working class, and it is such popular language all can understand. It gives them a place to start. Welcome, my Brothers and Sisters, my Comrades!

In my opinion, the problem now is to prepare for the Dictatorship of the Proletariat. If we are not properly prepared, the revisionists and those who are completely devoid of principle, technically referred to as opportunists, will merely see the revolution as an opportunity to seize political power. They will not hesitate, and if successful, will merely set themselves up as the new rulers. In response to those who think that the sheer power of the revolution will inspire those people to "turn over a new leaf", to act in a manner which is honest and principled, may I respond that perhaps you are confusing these people with the "Grinch Who Stole Christmas". It is best not to confuse the fantasy of children with reality. For that matter, it is difficult to separate the revisionists from those who are devoid of principle, possibly because the two are one and the same.

For that reason, I am encouraging all truly conscious people, Marxists, to come together and form an honest Communist Party, Dictatorship of the Proletariat. The most advanced members of the public, working class and middle class, are making a supreme effort, doing their best, trying to figure things out. Whether they know it or not, they are looking for leaders. That is your cue, feel free to act on it.

After the formation of the Party, then act as the leaders you are. Raise the level of awareness through encouraging the study of classic works of Marx, Engels and Lenin. Organize demonstrations and protests at "town halls" and primary meetings. Carry signs and banners which contain class content. Encourage workers to join the two mainstream political parties, to run for office on a state and federal level, to support Sanders, to demand the abolition of the Electoral College. This is the best way to train the proletariat for their approaching Dictatorship.

If all goes well, we will not have to make too many compromises with the unprincipled, the supposed Marxists, at the time of the revolution. The better prepared we are now for the revolution, the smoother will be the transition to the Dictatorship of the Proletariat.

As I have long maintained that the best way to get through to as many people as possible is through the use of slogans, may I suggest the following:

Unite the Left!
Sanders For President!
Join the Two Parties!
Scientific Socialism!
Workers of the World, Unite!

21

LEFT: STUDY MARXISM, JOIN THE 2 PARTIES!

Now that Super Tuesday, Round 2 is over, the press is reporting that the former Vice President, Joe Biden, is moving his campaign from possible "Democratic presidential contender" to "defeat Donald Trump" mode. He is putting out "peace feelers" to Senator Bernie Sanders, inviting Sanders to join him in opposition to Trump.

The press is also reporting that the Corona virus is now at the level of a pandemic, so that it has spread around the world. The whole country of Italy is now in "lockdown", with all public gatherings banned. In several countries of the world, all schools have been cancelled, among other things. As well, various parts of America are being "quarantined". The government authorities are going to the extreme length of not allowing fans to attend professional ball games. Even the NBA has cancelled all games "for the foreseeable future". Such a response is unprecedented, costing the capitalists a great deal of money.

As well, partly as a result of the Corona pandemic, the stock market has now officially entered "bear market territory".

Each day, the market "swings wildly", although the trend is downwards. It is reported that the capitalists have lost "trillions of dollars". Countless people are becoming sick and many are dying, and the only thing the capitalists can think about is their money!

One professional analyst, a truly starry eyed optimist, suggested that Trump should do something with which he is "not comfortable", and that was to be "honest with the American public". Someone should advise that misguided soul that it is not a matter of Trump being "comfortable" with the truth, but the simple fact of the matter is that Trump is simply a "stranger" to the truth. He is simply not capable of being honest. Trump lies constantly because that is simply his nature.

That same optimist thinks that perhaps Trump should bring together the country! As if, after a life of lies and deception, of treachery and intrigue, plotting and scheming to separate all and sundry from their hard earned money, Trump is now about to "turn over a new leaf" and play the role of Mother Theresa! That is not about to happen.

The simple fact of the matter is that these are the news items the press is reporting, and these are the same news items the members of the public, the working people, are hearing and talking about. At least, most members of the public watch the news. There are many working people who cannot bear to watch the news because it is too depressing. Those who do watch the news tend to find these events discouraging, at best.

The implication is that conscious people, which is to say Marxists, are not doing their duty. As the working class is not aware of itself as a class, it is not capable of developing class consciousness. This is fine by the ruling class, the monopoly capitalists, the bourgeoisie. They are supremely well aware of themselves as a class, just as they are equally well aware of the fact that the class opposite to them, the working class, the proletariat, is the source of all their wealth. The best way to exploit the proletariat, to "fleece the sheep", is to keep them "in the dark", unaware of the fact that they are members of a class, with their own class interests. In this, the bourgeoisie have succeeded rather well.

If there are any Marxists who are active in raising the level of awareness of the working class, they are doing a wonderful job of keeping a low profile. Perhaps they are afraid of bringing down the wrath of the capitalists upon their tender heads. Perhaps their fears are well founded. To this I can only respond that the internet has provided us with a valuable tool, one which we should use to its full capacity. It is possible to use the internet, post articles, appeal to the members of the working class, while remaining anonymous.

Then too, there are many well educated people, either current or former members of the middle class, who are supremely well aware of the revolutionary theories of Marx and Lenin, yet do not consider themselves to be Marxists. They may consider these theories to be mere curiosities, to which they are completely indifferent.

As well, there may be a number of working class people who have received a university education, and in the process, have learned those same theories, thus becoming class conscious. It matters not. The only thing that matter is their willingness to carry that class awareness, along with the Marxist revolutionary understanding, to the working class. The current revolutionary situation is now at the point where there is a desperate need for that awareness, among the working class. As this is all too frequently not happening, it is necessary to resort to alternative methods.

The working class is going to have to educate themselves! It is absolutely essential that the most advanced members of the working class read the most essential works of Marx, Engels and Lenin. I would suggest forming study groups, although it may not be necessary to get together physically. The various computer programs offer fine alternatives, such as getting together on skype, for example. Most working people are now literate, and have computers, or some such digital device. For those who are weak on computers, feel free to ask the advice of your children, as do I. They are sure to help us, if only at the expense of being called a "Caveman" or a "dinosaur". This in no way changes the fact that they love us. It is a small price to pay.

As previously mentioned, in other articles, I can suggest such key works as The Communist Manifesto, by Marx and Engels. Perhaps the most important work of Lenin is State and Revolution, as well as What Is To Be Done?, and Imperialism, the Highest Stage of Capitalism. That should give workers, those who are new to the revolutionary movement, a fine grounding in Marxist theories.

It is essential that a party be formed, one which can truly represent the working class, the proletariat. Of necessity, it must be exclusive, restricted to only the most dedicated revolutionaries, true followers of Marx and Lenin. I am suggesting the name of Communist Party, Dictatorship of the Proletariat, or CP,DP. It is only the true Marxists who call for the Dictatorship of the Proletariat. The phoney Marxists deny this necessity, or evade it, all in the service of the bourgeoisie. By openly advocating the Dictatorship of the Proletariat, we are distinguishing ourselves from those who claim to be Marxists, but are completely devoid of principle.

As yet, the vast majority of people, including the most advanced strata of the proletariat, have not embraced the scientific theories of Marx and Lenin. Many have not even heard of the Dictatorship of the Proletariat, although soon that will change. That in no way changes the fact that countless people are now politically active, taking an interest in their lives, determined to enact change. In that case, we can suggest that all Americans join the two mainstream political parties, Democratic and Republican, as card carrying members, "party bosses". It is free, open to all citizens.

It is the party bosses who set policy, and determine the individuals to run for any and all political office. The Americans who join the two parties will then be able to do as the capitalists suggest, which is to "change the system from within". They can nominate Leftist people for all offices, at a local, state and federal level. The capitals can be flooded with Leftist people, including Washington. Sanders can be nominated to run for president on behalf of both parties. The Electoral College can be abolished. All schools can be tuition free. All student loans can be abolished. All medical care can be free. The minimum wage can be increased. The pensions can be raised. No doubt seniors, students, workers and unemployed will be flocking to the two parties. Equally without doubt, the capitalists, the bourgeoisie, will have none of this.

This brings us to the current political situation, in that the press is reporting that Biden has a "commanding lead" over Sanders. That could change dramatically, if Leftist people get active! That includes not only joining the two parties, but to also hold demonstrations, carry signs and banners, disrupt primary meetings and town halls, demand the abolition of the Electoral College, demand a more fair and equitable democratic process. Insist on Sanders for president, on behalf of both parties!

As the women and students have proven themselves to be such excellent organizers in the recent past, they can no doubt do so again. Granted it is not fair to place this burden upon them, but then life is not fair. Under normal circumstances, the most advanced, highest paid members of the working class would assume this role, but as so many of them have been bribed by the capitalists, the burden is now on those people.

This is not to say that flooding Washington with Leftist people, including Sanders, will result in a socialist republic. It will not. The ruling class, the monopoly capitalists, the bourgeoisie, will never allow this. They will no doubt respond by changing their method of rule. At that time, they will "show their true colours", as is the popular expression. As a result of this, countless people, those whom honestly thought there could be a peaceful transition to socialism, will come to realize that we are right. Such people will then embrace scientific socialism, which is to say revolution and the subsequent Dictatorship of the Proletariat.

So on the one hand, we need a very small, exclusive group of people, true followers of Marx and Lenin, within the CP,DP. It is up to these people to raise the level of awareness of the members of the public, the working class, the proletariat, and the middle class, the petty bourgeois. In particular, the working class has to be made aware of itself as a class, with interests which are diametrically opposed to the class opposite to itself, the capitalist class, the bourgeoisie. The working class absolutely has to be made aware of the fact that it is destined to *overthrow the bourgeoisie and establish the Dictatorship of the Proletariat!*

On the other hand, we also need a very broad based coalition, from as many sections of the public as possible. This means working people and middle class people, as well as farmers. Most members of the middle class and farmers have been wiped out, forced into the ranks of the working class, but the remnants of those classes still exist. Even though they are rather few in number, we want them on our side. We can use all the help we can get!

The bourgeoisie has been in power for many years, and is deeply entrenched. They can and will be overthrown, but it will not be easy. Over the years, numerous efforts have been made, yet they remain in power. The one tactic which has not been employed against them is to "join them". By that I mean to hit them at the point where they are weakest, within the two parties. Destroy them from within.

As for those who are skeptical -I welcome such an attitude- may I suggest that there were possibly millions of Americans who marched at the inauguration of Trump, most of whom were women, and countless students also marched in their protest against being used for target practice. If all of those Americans choose to join the two parties, then I personally guarantee change.

I can also suggest that middle class intellectuals who are determined to enact change may consider forming a society of their choice. As members of that society, they can lobby the government for significant reforms. To each his own.

It is very likely that a broad spectrum of the population will choose to join the two parties. This includes people on the Left, as well as those on the Right. This is bound to create a certain amount of conflict. To those who are concerned, I can only respond that we place principle *before* personality. We do not have to love each other. We merely have to respect each other. When personalities clash, which is bound to happen on occasion, it is best to remind ourselves that our goal is to overthrow the bourgeoisie. A little irritation is a small price to pay.

We may also take comfort in the fact that our differences may lie with the leaders of various groups and factions, *but not with the rank and file!* This applies to people on both sides of the political spectrum, Left and Right. It is Abraham Lincoln who is credited with saying words to the effect that "the best way to destroy the enemy is to turn him into a friend."

Without doubt, experience is a fine teacher. Those on both sides of the political spectrum will soon realize that the bourgeoisie are not about to allow Americans to "change the system from within". They are in charge and fully intend to remain in charge. They are quite prepared to crush anyone who dares challenge their authority. That is the reason it is so important to come together, to have as broad a base as possible.

With that in mind, I will close my article with the usual slogans. When these slogans are widely seen on banners and posters, we will know we are reaching the American public.

Sanders For President!
Scientific Socialism!
Unite the Left!
Join the Two Parties!
Workers of the World, Unite!

22

TOO SMALL TO SUCCEED

The crisis in capitalism continues to intensify. The price of oil is now less than half of the lofty peak of that which it once occupied. The Corona virus has spread around the world, and various countries have responded by closing all sports events, religious gatherings, schools, malls and even their own borders. Citizens are being encouraged to "self isolate", to stay at home and avoid groups of "more than ten". It is not clear how members of large families are expected to do this.

As far as the capitalists are concerned, the situation is pretty grim. Not because people are getting sick and dying, but because those who "self isolate" are not spending their money. How can they? They are not allowed to travel or even go to the store. As a result of this, the profits of the capitalists are suffering. From the capitalist viewpoint, that is the real tragedy.

Experts in the field of health are reporting that the elderly, as well as those who are suffering from "preexisting conditions", are most at risk from from contracting the Corona virus. They are also reporting that young people may have the disease, while showing no symptoms. Such people are known as "carriers", those who spread the disease, through no fault of their own. Still, the health experts are encouraging young people to *not* get tested for the virus. Go figure.

Those same "health experts" are reporting that the death rate from those who contract the disease may vary from one to four percent, depending upon the level of medical treatment available. As it is anticipated that possibly half of the people in the country may soon be infected, it stands to reason that the death toll *could number in the millions.*

In response to this, Trump has just announced that "various health organizations are now working together in an unprecedented manner", in an attempt to develop a vaccine. It is doubtful that he realizes he has just announced a crushing condemnation of capitalism! He has effectively admitted that *under capitalism, even the health organizations do not cooperate!* They are in competition with each other, at the expense of the health, and even the life, of the citizens.

Health officials are reporting that we have reached a "tipping point", although they are careful not to explain what that means. Most simple souls consider a "tipping point" to be the point whereby a fluid overflows the side of a container, but clearly the health experts are using that expression to describe a phenomenon which they consider to be more elaborate, beyond the grasp of mere mortals.

The Treasury Secretary, Steve Mnuchin, is of the opinion that we can expect the unemployment rate to reach twenty percent, a rate not seen since the Great Depression. Not that we have to worry about another Depression, as the capitalists have refused to give a definition to the word! As a Depression is not defined, it ceases to exist. Impeccable logic!

The stock market reached "bear market territory" at the point where it lost twenty percent of its value, and has since lost another fifteen percent. The "financial experts" were asked if it could lose another thirty percent of its value, and the self described experts were clearly irritated at the question -the nerve of some people!- and were careful to avoid giving a straight answer.

The "health care workers" are concerned that the hospitals are facing a critical shortage of beds and ventilators. As those who are infected with the virus tend to experience "respiratory distress", or are short of breath, to phrase it in simple English, the use of ventilators can be the difference between life and death. These shortages are indeed serious.

It should come as no great surprise to anyone that our fearless leader, Donald Trump no less, is taking *no* responsibility for the crisis. As the wits phrase it, "the buck stops nowhere near the Oval Office". As president, he earlier said that the Corona virus would end by a "miracle", but as that has not happened, it is clear that the Lord has fallen down on the job, refusing to take orders from Trump. Imagine that.

The government is reporting that all "fiscal policy responses" have as yet failed to have any effect on the falling stock market. These "fiscal policy responses" include dropping the interest rates to effectively zero, and having the Federal Reserve "pump hundreds of billions of dollars" into the stock market.

It is note worthy that the financial experts are no longer talking in terms of billions, but in terms of *trillions*. It is reported that the Fed, as it is called, pumped a *trillion and a half* into the market, yet it had almost no effect. Now the government officials are talking about handouts to the tune of several trillion, national debt be damned! As Mnuchin just announced, the "economy will come roaring back". In a time of crisis, this is just what we need. A philosopher! Such starry eyed optimism will no doubt be a great comfort to those who are losing their jobs and life savings!

The capitalists are concerned, to the point of being frantic, with the financial state of the major airlines. It is being reported -shock and horror!- that those companies could go broke within a couple months, unless they receive a massive "capital infusion". In other words, the politicians are desperate to "bail them out", to give them a huge "handout", although they "bend over backwards" in an attempt to avoid using these terms. My personal favourite is the reference to corporate welfare as "increasing liquidity". As a result of this, the politicians have determined to bless them with an initial gift of possibly fifty billion, with many more billions to follow, along with tax breaks. Of course, other major companies, such as those involved in various tourism industries, including the cruise ship industry, hotel chains and restaurants, will also be smiled upon by the government. By contrast, small business owners can expect to receive a great deal of sympathy. Try taking that to the bank!

Among the capitalists, it is understood that some businesses are 'Too Big To Fail", while other companies, as well as individuals, are 'Too Small To Succeed". This is not to say that Trump is completely heartless, indifferent to the suffering of the "little guy". On the contrary, he has graciously agreed to "suspend all home foreclosures and evictions". This should come as a great comfort to those who are about to lose their jobs and houses and join the ranks of the homeless. It has been delayed for a certain time! Gee thanks, Mister Billionaire President! You are too kind!

The braver of the capitalist analysts are predicting that a "shutdown is inevitable", businesses should send all non essential employees home, and that we are entering a "depression era period". As the "Big Three" American automakers are reported to have just shut down, and the Las Vegas casinos are apparently following suit, that conclusion is something less than a stroke of genius. No doubt those corporations, including the gambling establishments, those which take such great delight in separating us from our hard earned money, will also qualify for a government handout!

As I write this, it has just been reported that all the gains of the stock market, which has been made since Trump was elected, have been erased. The stock market has now lost 35 percent of its value. This is not to say that Trump is indifferent to the suffering of the common people, the "little guy". In fact, he is graciously planning to send a check of one thousand dollars, a "grand", or possibly more, to all citizens. Those who receive this bonus can use it to buy an old car, to be used as a shelter, as a replacement for the home they are about to lose. In this way, they can join the ranks of those who are homeless and forced to live in their cars. There is no shortage of such people, and they are among the more fortunate. The less fortunate are forced to live under bridges.

In fact, the proposed "grand hand out" is nothing more than an added humiliation, a mere addition to the degradation of being unemployed and homeless.

To put this financial downturn in scientific terms, it is a fundamental tenet of Marxism that a commodity sells for the cost of production. This means that for a while, a commodity will sell for a price above the cost of production, and there is great joy in the land of capital, or at least Wall Street, because business is making a profit. Then there comes a surplus, the price of the commodity drops, and it sells for a loss. Doom and gloom reigns on Wall Street. There is weeping and wailing in the land of capital. Even the capitalists admit that business proceeds in a "boom to bust cycle", yet at the same time they expect the stock market to merely rise steadily. Each time the market takes a dip, the capitalists lose money, and they are shocked. This merely proves the fact that the capitalists are masters of self delusion.

As for those who think that these fluctuations in the stock market should level out under this stage of capitalism, monopoly capitalism, which is referred to as imperialism, you are mistaken. As Lenin stated quite clearly, if not emphatically: "The statement that cartels can abolish crises is a fable spread by bourgeois economists whom at all costs desire to place capitalism in a favourable light. On the contrary, when monopoly appears in *certain* branches of industry, it increases and intensifies the anarchy inherent in capitalist production as a *whole*." (italics by Lenin)

As I write this, for the first time since the birth of the latest capitalist crisis, the press is now using the "D word", which is to say Depression. The implication is that the crisis is quite severe, and the Corona virus is anticipated to last for possibly eighteen months. As long as it lasts, we can expect people to "self isolate", if for no other reason than that they have no choice. At the same time, those same people will not be at work producing, or shopping, or travelling, or spending their money, if only because they do not have money to spend. It stands to reason that profits will suffer.

Strangely enough, the more optimistic stock brokers, die hard capitalists one and all, are practically yelling at investors to "stay the course". Perhaps they feel that by "raising the volume", investors will be more impressed. Or perhaps they are merely wired on some good drugs. They are going to need such drugs, and lots of them.

This brings us to the rational souls who are pointing out that the country is deeply in debt, to the tune of *23 trillion dollars*, and that is merely the amount the federal government admits to owing. The real amount is not mentioned. These sane individuals question the sanity of going far deeper into debt. The response is that now is not the time to quibble over the national debt! This is similar to the expression "damn the torpedoes, full speed ahead!" Those are famous last words. Torpedoes are not damned. Torpedoes do the damning. Those who challenge torpedoes do not often live to regret it.

In much the same way, fool hardy souls can ignore the national debt. The national debt will not ignore the country. The people who own the national debt, those who are technically referred to as members of the bourgeoisie, will demand payments on that debt. What is more, they will receive payment, if only because they are members of the ruling class. Even though the tax base is shrinking, because businesses are closing and individuals are losing their jobs, the interest payments on the national debt must continue. This can and will be done, but only at the expense of such little details as disability pensions, old age pensions, hospitals, schools, clinics, libraries, play grounds, national parks, police and fire protection, and so forth. Regardless of how difficult the depression becomes, the bourgeoisie are determined that they will not lose a dime. They never lost a dime in the first Great Depression, and they have no intention of breaking with that tradition now.

With that in mind, the press is reporting that various small business owners are looking at bankruptcy. No doubt this is true, as the capitalist monopolies become ever more complete. Ever more small business owners, referred to as petty bourgeois, are being forced into the ranks of the working class, the proletariat. That is merely a fact, just as it is a fact that those same people bring with them the class awareness, which is foreign to the proletariat.

In this article, I have gone to considerable length in quoting from press reports. I have also expressed myself in popular language, using colloquialisms which common people can understand. The reason for this is that common people watch the news, and in fact they watch it religiously. They then discuss it among themselves, trying to make sense of this. They also read, and in fact they read a great deal. The trouble is that they are limited in their comprehension due to the fact that *the working class is not aware of itself as a class!*

I most passionately hope that members of the working class are reading this article. To such people I can only say that I am writing this, with you in mind. You, as the members of the proletariat, must become class conscious. You must overthrow the ruling class, the bourgeoisie, and crush them under the Dictatorship of the Proletariat. This can only be done through revolution, and this requires the correct Marxist leadership. Otherwise, those who are devoid of principle, referred to as opportunists, will merely set themselves up as the new rulers.

Bear in mind that this class awareness can only come from members of the middle class, so do not hold the class background of an individual against them. Marx and Engels were members of the middle class, for example. Each of them could have chosen to live a comfortable bourgeois life style, but chose to do the right thing. They devoted their lives to the service of the working people, proletariat, peasant and petty bourgeois.

We can expect those who are current or former members of the middle class to bring the class awareness to the working class, the proletariat, but do not count on this. As yet, this has not been happening, or at least not in sufficient quantity. Not to despair, the works of Marx and Lenin are readily available, or at least the most essential works. With that in mind, I encourage all workers to read The Communist Manifesto by Marx and Engels, State and Revolution by Lenin, What Is To Be Done? by Lenin, and Imperialism, the Highest Stage of Capitalism, by Lenin. A careful reading of those works will give workers a solid grounding in scientific socialism, other wise known as Marxism.

I am sure that everyone, working class as well as middle class, will now agree with me when I say that the situation is now at a critical point. It continues to intensify, with the rich, the bourgeoisie, becoming ever richer, and the common people, the working class, the proletariat, as well as the middle class, the petty bourgeois, becoming ever more poor. In fact, ever more members of the middle class are becoming ruined, their businesses are going under, as the capitalists consider them Too Small To Succeed. The government handouts are strictly for the major corporations, those who are Too Big To Fail.

Now it is up to middle class intellectuals, including those who have been forced into the ranks of the working class, to share your understanding of the awareness of classes, including the Marxist necessity of revolution and the subsequent Dictatorship of the Proletariat.

Bear in mind that time is not on our side. The revolution could break out any day now. I will close this article with my usual slogans, as they are so important:

Workers of the World, Unite!
Scientific Socialism!
Dictatorship of the Proletariat!

23

DEPRESSION AND THE FEDERAL RESERVE

The Corona virus has now spread around the world, which is to say that it is now at pandemic levels. If it was confined to a single country, it would be referred to as an epidemic. I mention this for the benefit of those who are not clear concerning the subject. This pandemic is being blamed for the crisis in capitalism, the collapse of the global economy, which is now being referred to as a depression. Such is not the case. This depression is the natural result of capitalism, precisely as predicted by Marx.

It has been reported that the country of Italy has been very hard hit by the virus, with possibly 6,500 deaths so far. The whole country is in a state of "lockdown", with good reason. The medical personnel are doing their best, at great risk to themselves, with the equipment which is available. It is reported that the medical professionals are exhausted and desperate. It is very likely that a similar situation will soon be faced by the citizens of America, as the United States is expected to become the latest epicentre of the pandemic.

Within the country, New York City is considered to be the "centre of the epidemic". The number of people who are now known to have the virus has "sky rocketed", if for no other reason than that more people are now being tested for the virus. In many cases, people who have the virus show no symptoms. These same people spread the virus, through no fault of their own. Such people are known as carriers. It only makes sense to isolate people, to exercise "social distancing", as a means of containing the virus.

As I write this, perhaps one third of the American people are being told to stay at home, unless they absolutely have to leave their houses for essential service jobs. Even then, they are being advised to stay a safe distance from each other, six feet or two meters.

The Surgeon General, Dr. Jerome Adams, says "this week, it is going to get bad". As he is the top medical professional in the country, all would be well advised to listen carefully to that which he says. That includes President Trump, who has his own ideas. It should come as no surprise to anyone to learn that Trump is "at odds with the medical profession". He clearly thinks that he knows more about the medical situation than the medical professionals. But then it is not reasonable to expect anything better from someone who is so supremely ignorant.

This in no way changes the fact that the medical professionals are treating patients who are infected with the Corona virus, at great personal risk to themselves. The only thing they are asking for in return is the proper "personal protective equipment, or PPE". By that they mean masks, gowns and surgical gloves. In addition, the patients who are desperately sick, short of breath, need ventilators. There is a severe shortage of ventilators, just as there is a shortage of hospital beds.

These are the facts, just as it is also a fact that Trump is fond of giving speeches, even at press conferences. That is a man who loves the sound of his own voice! At these conferences, and in front of his medical advisers, no less, he states things which directly contradict the opinion of those same medical professionals. As one of them stated it, "I can't jump in front of the microphone and push him down." No doubt the temptation is do so is very strong. At least the thought is most pleasant.

The frustration of the medical professionals does not end there. As president, Trump did exercise his authority to activate the Defence Production Act, which gives him the authority to force businesses to produce medical equipment. Ordinarily, this Act is used as a means of forcing industry to produce war material. Now it is being used to force the same industry to produce medical supplies. Or more accurately, *it could* be used for that purpose, but it is not. Now that Trump has activated that Act, he refuses to enforce it. Industry can produce such medical items or not, as they see fit. For the moment, they see fit to *not* produce such items. Perhaps the profit margin is not sufficient to justify the expense of retooling the factories. This is the way the capitalists think. As Trump is a capitalist, this he understands.

As I write this, it has just been reported that the stock market is down from its all time high by 37 percent, or just over a third. For some strange reason, the reporters are of the opinion that those of us who watch the news are half Philadelphia lawyers and half rocket scientists. I mention this for the sake of the odd viewer who is neither, is not familiar with percentages, and is not even a mathematician. They also mention that the market is on track for having its worst month since 1931, at the height of the Great Depression. That is not a coincidence.

This is not to say that our fearless leader, Donald Trump, is indifferent to the suffering of American citizens. Indeed not. He has given it a great deal of thought and come to the conclusion that "the cure cannot be worse than the sickness". He has therefore decided that the country must be re-opened for business, that all shutdowns must end, that the six foot exclusion rule must be tossed, and the pandemic will be over within the next few weeks. President Trump is truly a man of action! In fact, he wants the country "opened up and just raring to go by Easter". In fact, he announced this on the very day the daily death toll from the Corona virus reached a record high.

If nothing else, this provides all of us with a very clear cut setting for the class war. And it is a war, with the "lower classes", which is to say the working class, the proletariat, in partnership with the family farmers, as well as the middle class, the petty bourgeois, against the monopoly capitalist class, the bourgeoisie. The capitalists have made their position quite clear. Their spokesman, Donald Trump, no less, is more concerned with the economy than with the fact that countless people are getting sick and dying!

Think of it. The medical professionals are of the opinion that the pandemic is about to "become much worse", that the "worst is yet to come", that we have a "desperate shortage of medical equipment", everything from "personal protective equipment to ventilators", and the only thing the capitalists are concerned about is their *profit!* It has been reported that *two million* people applied for unemployment benefits in *one week*, and it is anticipated that another *seven million* will soon join the ranks of the unemployed, and yet the press is focused on the *stock market!*

As the news outlets are owned and operated by the capitalists, this is understandable, and we should not blame the journalists for reporting on that which concerns the capitalists. They are merely doing their job, and many of them sneak in news tidbits as best they can. This in no way changes the fact that the capitalists are deeply concerned with the stock market, as that is a reflection of their profits. As the stock markets are plunging, the capitalists are responding by "propping up the markets". In fact, the Federal Reserve Board, otherwise known as the Fed, has pumped countless billions of dollars, even *trillions*, into the market, as well as reducing the interest rates to effectively zero. This they refer to as "economic stimulus", and the markets have responded by continuing to drop. In fact, some economists expect the market to lose another third of its value, reducing the country to depression levels, not seen since the Great Depression.

As all measures to stop the decline of the stock market have had almost no effect, the capitalists have decided to pump more money into the market. As anyone with a lick of sense could tell them, it has not worked before and is not about to work now. But then capitalists are convinced that money solves all problems. Any evidence to the contrary is quietly ignored.

This bring us to the "Fed", the Federal Reserve Board. Countless people have heard of this outfit, and it clearly has great power, so it stands to reason to look into this secretive organization. The people on this Board control the "Federal Reserve System", the "central banking system of the United States of America". It was reportedly "created by Congress to provide the nation with a safer, more flexible and more stable monetary and financial system". As the economy of the country is now in free fall, it is safe to say that it has fallen short of this noble objective.

The key component of the Fed is the Federal Reserve Bank, the "nations central bank, an agency of the federal government and reports to and is directly accountable to the Congress... the Fed has control of the money supply through its power to create credit, with interest rates and reserve requirements." It does not take an economist to realize that the Fed has incredible power.

Yet there is more to it than that. The Congress has decided that the Fed has four functions. The first is to manage the inflation rate at preferably 2 percent, and to keep prices stable. The effect of inflation is to gradually lower the standard of living of the working class, as wage increases rarely keep up with inflation. This means that in the past, such as immediately after the Second World War, it was customary for a family to have one parent working, usually the father, while the mother stayed home and raised the children. That is now a thing of the past, the "good old days", which they were not, but working people did enjoy a higher standard of living. As a result of inflation, our standard of living has dropped considerably, so it is safe to say that the Fed has achieved its goal of reducing the standard of living of the working class. It is also safe to say that the Fed has failed miserably in its goal of keeping prices stable.

The second goal of the Fed is to "supervise and regulate many of the nations banks to protect consumers". This begs the question, what do they mean by "consumer"? If they are referring to the fellow capitalists, then the Fed is performing a magnificent job. If they are referring to the common people, then that is a different story completely. But of course the only concern of the capitalists is with other capitalists.

The third role of the Fed is to "maintain the stability of the financial markets and constrain potential crises". Any way you look at this, the Fed has also failed miserably, in this objective. The "financial markets", by which we can only assume they mean the stock market, is in free fall, the unemployment rate is expected to hit 20 percent, countless small businesses are expected to close, and the country is entering a depression, one which is expected to be even more intense than the Great Depression. So much for "constraining potential crises!"

The fourth role of the Fed is to "provide banking services to other banks, the US government and foreign banks". The income of this bank is "derived primarily from interest earned on US government securities that the Federal Reserve has acquired through open market operations."

The economists are concerned now, as the Fed has placed all their money -and then some- into the stock market, in an attempt to prop it up. The results are clear for all to see. The most kind and considerate of the economists refer to the stock market as "volatile", in that it may "rise one day and fall two days". It has been compared to a roller coaster, with the trend downwards.

As a result of this, the economists are warning that the "entire global financial system is at a tremendous level of risk. Governments could conceivably be facing bankruptcy."

It is not too often that economists blurt out something completely honest, but this is one such rare event. As that is the case, perhaps we can pause and cherish the moment.

Now that the pause is over, let us face the fact that even the bourgeois economists are facing the fact that the Federal Reserve Bank is on the verge of bankruptcy! If that happens -when that happens?- various governments around the world, including the United States of America, are anticipated to *go broke!*

The capitalists have not yet exhausted their bag of tricks. The leaders of both parties, of both houses of Congress, the Senate and House of Representatives, are currently in negotiations, trying to "hammer out a deal" of possibly more than *two trillion dollars,* in an attempt to "stimulate the economy". One of those leaders has reported "broad bipartisan support" and that "conceptually we are there". By way of translation, this is "bourgeois speak" for the fact that they are "at each others throats", no where near agreement. The press is reporting that behind closed doors, they are not even civil with each other.

The more passionate supporters of the bourgeoisie are determined to give hundreds of billions of taxpayer money to the biggest, richest, most powerful corporations, those who are "Too Big To Fail". This includes the major airlines, auto manufacturers, hotel chains, restaurant chains, ocean cruise chains, computer manufacturers and casinos. Small companies, which are described as those who employ less than 500 people, as well as individuals, are "Too Small To Succeed". As far as the capitalists are concerned, the rest of us can go the way of the dodo bird.

This stands in sharp contrast to other voices, those who are possibly *even more passionate supporters of the bourgeoisie!* They are determined that this "economic stimulus package" should go to the "little guy", which is to say the small business owner and the working people, especially those who are losing their jobs. They would like to see a check sent to all Americans, as well as "Unemployment Insurance on Steroids", so that those who are out of work will receive their full income, at least for a short time.

No doubt the reason for this benevolent attitude, coming from those who are the most avid supporters of the bourgeoisie, has nothing to do with concern for the "common people", the "little guy". They are just well aware that the working class is in motion, demanding change, becoming aware of themselves as a class, politically active. These people have "their ear to the ground", are well aware that a revolt is brewing, a full scale revolution could break out any day now, and "drastic steps" must be taken to forestall that revolution. Their idea of drastic steps is to send a little money to the working people, to "throw a few coppers to the Natives", to effectively "buy people off". As if a few paltry dollars will stop the revolution!

I have news for all of you, those of you who are belly crawling boot lickers of the bourgeoisie. We are not our grandparents. We are not about to put up with all the crap our grandparents put up with. This is not 1929 and this depression is not about to drag on for ten years and end with a war. We are well aware that there are over *six hundred billionaires* in the country, and they are all living "high off the hog". We also know that those people are monopoly capitalists, imperialists, members of the class of people whom are technically referred to as the bourgeoisie. They are the members of the ruling class, responsible for this depression, this crisis in capitalism. This depression is proof that capitalism does not work. To suggest that this depression came about as a result of the Corona virus is nonsense. This depression came about as a result of capitalism, pure and simple, just as predicted by Marx.

The current situation is exceptionally sharp and clear. The last of the middle class, the petty bourgeois, the small business owner, is now facing bankruptcy, being forced into the ranks of the working class, the proletariat. Now in America, there is effectively no middle class! It is a war of the monopoly capitalist, the billionaires, the bourgeoisie, against the working class, the proletariat. There is no longer any vacillating petty bourgeois to "muddy the waters", to confuse the issue with their petty bourgeois mentality. They no longer exist.

It is a fundamental tenet of Marxism that the proletariat is destined to overthrow the bourgeoisie, smash the existing state apparatus and establish the Dictatorship of the Proletariat. Before long, the working class will rise up in revolt, but spontaneously, as it is not yet aware of itself as a class, complete with its own class interests. Still less is it aware of its destiny to crush the bourgeoisie under the Dictatorship of the Proletariat. It is absolutely essential that the proletariat be made aware of this, and it is the duty of every conscious person, every scientific socialist, by which I of course mean

Marxist, to carry this awareness to the proletariat. The best way to do this -if not the only way- is through the leadership which can only be provided by a party. I am of course suggesting the name Communist Party, Dictatorship of the Proletariat, or CP,DP, as a means of distinguishing ourselves from the parties which claim to be Marxist, but are not.

I am also suggesting that all Americans be encouraged to join the two mainstream political parties, Democrat and Republican, as card carrying members, party bosses. As such, they will get to decide the individuals to run for any and all political offices, will be able to flood Washington and state capitals with Leftist people, can work to abolish the Electoral College, increase the minimum wage, abolish all student loans, increase the pensions, defend our democratic rights, and in the process, will receive most valuable training for the Dictatorship of the Proletariat. They will learn first hand that the bourgeoisie are in charge, and fully intend to remain in charge.

In summary, I am suggesting an extremely exclusive Communist Party, an organization of dedicated Marxists, those who are committed to revolution and the subsequent Dictatorship of the Proletariat. The members of this Party can focus on raising the level of awareness of the working class, especially the most advanced workers, to that of the level of Marxists. These people will know they are making progress when the term Dictatorship of the Proletariat is commonly discussed among working people.

I am also suggesting a very broad based coalition of Leftist people, which would include anyone and everyone who is the slightest bit interested in defending our democratic rights. They should be encouraged to join the two mainstream political parties. This of course includes seniors, students, workers, unemployed and homeless. In fact, everyone who is dissatisfied with the current political situation, in which a handful of people live in extreme wealth, while the vast majority live in extreme poverty. The more advanced will run for political office, or at least make the attempt. In this manner, they will receive valuable training in leadership, which will serve them well after the revolution, when such workers will be placed in key positions, within the newly created Dictatorship of the Proletariat.

No doubt this latest crisis in capitalism, this depression, will help to motivate conscious people, Marxists, to form a proper Communist Party. Equally without doubt, it will also inspire people to take action, to join the two mainstream political parties. It is to be hoped that it will also motivate certain people, by whom I am of course referring to the leaders of the Womens' March, as well as the Students Protest Movement, to once again become active. I have complete confidence in you. You have done it before and you can do it again. The difference this time is to *not* focus on narrow issues, but to focus on capitalism and the class of capitalists, the bourgeoisie. They can and must be destroyed.

With that in mind, I will close this article with my usual suggestions for slogans. I mention these slogans as they are so important. It is the best way to raise the level of awareness of the working class. It gives people a place to start.

Scientific Socialism!
Dictatorship of the Proletariat!
Workers of the World, Unite!

24

ECONOMIC STIMULUS PACKAGE- HA!

The country is currently entering a depression such as has not been seen since the Great Depression of almost one hundred years ago. The more honest of the bourgeois economists admit this, while qualifying the statement that this depression is expected to be more intense. In fact, they cannot see any way out of this depression, this crisis in capitalism, if only because there is none.

This has not stopped the monopoly capitalists, the imperialists, the bourgeoisie, from making an attempt. They have come up with a two trillion dollar -that is two thousand billion dollar-" economic stimulus package". This is tax payer money, which they do not have, which is being given away to citizens and businesses. Each American will receive a rather small check, that of their own taxpayer money, while the vast majority, the" lions share", will go to businesses. This is known as" corporate welfare".

These corporate welfare checks, to some of the biggest corporations in the country, as well as to" small businesses", are supposed to prop up these companies until the corona virus" runs its course", and things "return to normal". In the simplicity of their souls, the capitalists have defined any business which employs less than 500 workers as a" small business." Small business, indeed!

The idea is that the owner of a" small business" will trust this" mild recession" to be over in the third quarter, with a recovery" later in the year", as was predicted by a top economist. Accordingly, it is expected that this starry eyed optimistic businessman will keep paying his workers, even though they are idle, as well as paying the rent, utilities and taxes on all his stock and supplies, patiently waiting for the corona virus to run its course, the country to "get back on its feet", and customers to return. This begs the question: Just how stupid does the government think these" small business owners"are?

All such business people are small time capitalists, petty bourgeois. This is not to suggest that they are entirely stupid, as they are not. They are well aware that it is the opinion of the more honest economists that we are entering a depression, things will never again return to "normal", and it is therefore time to "cash in their chips", otherwise known as "liquidating", "cut their losses", and "run like hell". In other words, they will fire their workers, close up shop, sell whatever they can for as much as they can, throw away the rest, and if need be, file for bankruptcy. At the same time, they will grab as much cash as they can, including the government handouts. They would be fools to do anything less.

I have deliberately phrased this in very popular language, so that the average working person can understand it. It is very important. We are entering a depression, and we had best be prepared for the worst.

Allow me to stress that this crisis in capitalism, this depression, did not come about as a result of the corona virus. It is a natural result of the development of capitalism. As Marx pointed out, capitalism proceeds in a natural cycle of boom to bust. The boom is over, the bust is here, it is worldwide, and in my opinion, there is no way the capitalists are going to get out of this one.

This brings us to the corporate executives, the" big business" people. These are the people who control whole branches of industry, which include airlines, hotel chains, auto manufacturers, restaurant chains and various other branches of business. The idea that they are prepared to get their hands on ten and even hundreds of billions of dollars -this they refer to as capital- and waste it on" stimulating the economy" -well, let's just say that the thought would never occur to them. It would simply never cross their mind. Instead, they are sure to look for opportunities elsewhere, probably overseas, with the idea of getting a better return on their invested capital. Bear in mind, this" capital" is nothing more than American tax payer money, which has generously been donated to them, by Trump and the Washington politicians.

As a result of this" economic stimulus package", the country is being driven ever deeper into depression, ever closer to bankruptcy.

This in no way changes the fact that the most immediate, pressing concern, is that of dealing with the corona virus. The United States now has the dubious distinction of being the country with the greatest number of reported cases of people infected with the corona virus. The American medical system is in danger of collapse! The health care workers are exhausted. Many have come out of retirement to assist in the crisis. They are scrambling for personal protective equipment, risking their health, in danger of contracting the virus and spreading it to others, their families as well as other patients. There is a desperate shortage of ventilators. Refrigerator trucks are being pressed into service, in order to store the corpses, as the morgues are filled to overflowing. The hospitals are expected to run out of beds in a few days. They are expected to need over twice as many beds as they have now. The doctors are describing the situation in the hospitals as" apocalyptic".

As that is the case, the governors of the states which are most hard hit by the virus are appealing to the federal government for help. In other words, they are appealing to Donald Trump! There is no one more indifferent to their suffering than Donald Trump! His main concern, if not his only concern, is to funnel as much tax payer money as possible to the members of his class, the monopoly capitalists, the billionaires, the bourgeoisie. The suffering of the" little guy", the" common people", does not concern him.

In all fairness, it is true that Trump has activated the Defense Production Act, which gives him the authority to force businesses to produce emergency medical equipment, such as personal protective equipment, hospital beds and ventilators, among other items which are so desperately needed. He activated this Act under great pressure, but is reluctant to use it. The last thing he wants to do is to force corporations to produce such articles, as this" smack of socialism".

In this, he has a point. Under socialism, or at least under scientific socialism, people are placed before profits! This stands in sharp contrast to capitalism, especially under the current state of medical emergency, where it is clear for all to see, that profits are placed before people!

It is very likely that Trump, as well as the journalists who report such news items, are not aware that they are condemning the system of capitalism!

The journalists are torn between reporting the devastation caused by the deepening depression, the havoc caused by the corona virus, and the glowing economic forecasts of the officials who serve the capitalists so fervently. The Treasury Secretary, Steve Mneuchin, says that the 3,280,000 new jobless claims, in merely one week, are" not relevant", that the" fundamentals of the economy remain strong". Tell that to the people who are now unemployed! Tell that to the millions more who are about to become unemployed!

Trump is living in his own little dream world, far removed from reality.

His latest brain storm is to classify counties under new guide lines, that of" low risk, medium risk and high risk". The level of risk will in turn determine the degree of" social distancing", so that the economy can "come roaring back in time for Easter". Perhaps he should relocate from the White House to the insane asylum.

In all fairness to Trump, he is aided in his delusions by the bourgeois belly crawling boot lickers. There is no shortage of the vermin, and they go to great lengths, even absurd lengths, to protect their lords and masters, the bourgeoisie. The Chairman of the Federal Reserve has announced that" we may well be in a recession". He went on to say that he expects a" robust recovery in the fourth quarter". To think that this is announced, by one of the most highly respected economists in the country, at the beginning of a depression!

At the rate the corona virus is spreading, it is very likely that soon, people will be dying while waiting to be admitted to hospitals. The hospital staff cannot provide them with beds which they do not have. Nor can they place them on ventilators, when they have no ventilators. It is doubtful that the family members, those who are mourning the loss of their loved ones, will take a great deal of comfort in the fact that the corporations were not forced to manufacture these medical items, as that smacks of socialism!

There is a limit to that which people are prepared to tolerate, and the American people are close to that limit. We are entering a depression, the corona virus is ravaging the country, common people are suffering terribly, the country is on the verge of bankruptcy, the medical system is about to collapse, and the only thing the government can think about is stimulating the economy!

It is clear that their idea of" stimulating the economy" is merely giving the super-rich, the billionaires, the bourgeoisie, ever more billions! The country can go" down the tubes", but as long as the billionaires amass an even greater fortune, that is perfectly acceptable!

The differences now are at least sharp and clear. As Dickens would say," it was the best of times, it was the worst of times".

He was of course referring to the situation in France at the time of the French revolution, in which the nobility never had it so good -the best of times- and the" lower classes", the peasants and workers, never had it so bad -the worst of times.

A similar situation now exists in America. In this country, the nobility was overthrown many years ago, but they have been replaced by the bourgeoisie, a class which is every bit as reactionary as the nobility. The peasants are almost completely wiped out, and now the middle class, the petty bourgeois, is following suit, being forced into the ranks of the working class, the proletariat. One difference between America of today and France at the time of Dickens, is the fact that the class conflict is now much simpler. Now there is essentially two classes, the working class or proletariat, and the capitalist class, or bourgeoisie. All other classes have been destroyed.

The country is a" powder keg", set to explode. A spontaneous uprising, a revolution, could break out any day. As yet, the working class is not aware of itself as a class, not aware that it is at war with the capitalist class, the bourgeoisie. This awareness can only come from Marxists. It is up to Marxists to make the proletariat aware of the fact that it is destined to overthrow the bourgeoisie, smash the existing state apparatus and crush that class of parasites, the billionaires, the bourgeoisie, under the Dictatorship of the Proletariat.

As yet, the Marxists are not providing that service. For that reason, I can suggest that working people who are reading this article make haste to educate yourselves. Time is not on our side, so by all means, read the Essential Works of Lenin.

That should provide workers with a solid background in Marxist theory.

A Communist Party is desperately needed. It must be exclusive, restricted to only the most dedicated Marxists, those who are committed to revolution and the subsequent Dictatorship of the Proletariat.

During the time of revolution, leaders will emerge. These leaders will be true Marxists or they will be totally unprincipled, those committed to seizing the opportunity to set themselves up as the new rulers. As we live in a class society, those are the options. Proletarian or bourgeois, there is no middle ground.

Now that this depression is destroying so many members of the petty bourgeois, the middle class, perhaps those among you who are Marxists will become active and carry the message to the working class. That is up to you. Bear in mind that in a revolution, no one can remain" neutral", or" straddle the fence". The last thing you want is to become a target of the revolution.

In summary, the" battle lines are being drawn". It is workers versus billionaires, proletariat versus bourgeoisie. Socialism or capitalism, a war to the finish. No quarter. Victory or death. The working class has nothing to lose but its chains.

25

ICHTHYOSAUR IN OKANAGAN LAKE?

There have been numerous sightings of an animal in Okanagan Lake, a huge animal which local residents refer to as" Ogopogo". Most of these sightings are consistent and reliable, made by people who are highly respected. There is every reason to believe that the animal exists. Now the problem is one of proving it.

First a little background is in order. It is the scientific opinion that many millions of years ago, there were an additional four orders of swimming reptiles in the world. Within each order, there were likely dozens of species. These orders were that of ichthyosaur, mosasaur, long necked plesiosaur and short necked plesiosaur. Then around 80 million years ago, or mya for short, the ichthyosaurs went extinct, due to competition from other" super predators", possibly mosasaurs. It is further the scientific opinion that the other three orders of swimming reptile went extinct 65 million years ago, at the same time the dinosaurs went extinct. No reason is given for the mass extinctions of these swimming reptiles.

It is my opinion that the scientists are" all wet", if you will excuse the poor joke. I am convinced that these four orders of swimming reptiles still exist, predators one and all, in the lakes and oceans of the world.

For the benefit of those readers who are not scientists, I will mention that an" order" is a reference to a group of species of animals which are quite similar. For example, there is an order of crocodiles, and that order includes twenty-three species. By contrast, within the order of turtles, there are possibly one hundred species. Both crocodiles and turtles are swimming reptiles, but the difference is that turtles can tolerate a great deal of cold, while crocodiles cannot. Hence the great many species of turtle, as compared to the relatively few species of crocodile.

To return to the animal in Okanagan Lake, the most reliable eye witness reports are that it swims like a mammal, not a reptile. They mention this because they are well aware that reptiles swim in an undulating manner, while mammals swim in a completely different manner. I believe them. They also report that this animal has" humps" on its back, which go up and down as it swims. This too I believe. Making sense of these reports is a different matter entirely.

Perhaps the most surprising report was that of the swimmer who found himself swimming with company! A huge animal was swimming right alongside of him! As it was so close, it was difficult not to notice the huge eyes on the animal, eyes the size of grapefruits!

It is details such as this which help to determine the identity of the animal. The one and only swimming reptile with such huge eyes, possibly 25 centimeters or 10 inches, is the ichthyosaur.

This called for a little investigation on my part, in an attempt to reconcile the behavior. The swimming motion of this animal is that of a mammal, and to swim alongside a human is also characteristic of a mammal, and in particular that of a dolphin. No reptile has been known to exhibit such behavior. Yet the ichthyosaur is classified as a reptile.

Strangely enough, even though it is a reptile, the fossilized remains of the ichthyosaur confirm that this animal gives birth to live young. It is characteristic of reptiles that they lay eggs, although rattle snakes are the exception, giving birth to live young. Apparently, these ichthyosaurs are also the exception.

It is also the scientific opinion that this animal is related to dolphins. I have no idea how they came to that conclusion, but I am sure they are right. As far as I am aware, dolphins are the only swimming animals which have been known to swim alongside people. At least, up until now. Something is swimming alongside people in Okanagan Lake, and it is not a dolphin.

The idea that a reptile, a super predator no less, would choose to swim alongside a human, is stranger than fiction.

Further investigation reveals that the latest scientific discoveries question the belief that the ichthyosaur is a cold-blooded animal. If it is indeed a warm-blooded animal -and that has yet to be prove- one which gives birth to live young, then it may be improperly classified. It may be a RINO, a

Reptile in Name Only. It may in fact be a mammal, and that would explain its mammalian behavior.

This is not to say that I am terribly concerned with the classification of the animal. It can be a reptile with mammalian characteristics, or it can be a mammal with reptilian characteristics. It is a subject upon which I am indifferent. No doubt the proper classification is important, but I am mainly concerned with proving the existence of the animal.

Ordinarily I would say that the best way to prove the existence of a swimming reptile is by locating its nesting site, the beach upon which it lays its eggs. But this is anything but ordinary, as it gives birth to live young. There is no point in looking for the beach where it lays its eggs, because that beach does not exist. Clearly, it is necessary to come up with a different plan.

The people who have seen these animals are of the opinion that they are most frequently seen in the spring, at certain locations. Possibly the males come to the surface and display, in an attempt to impress the females. Who can blame them?

Assuming that to be the case, may I suggest that those who live around Okanagan Lake keep an eye out for these animals, and hopefully git some pictures, preferably videos, of those animals cavorting in the water. There was a time when an animal had to be killed, in order to prove the species exists. I would like to prove to the scientists that this animal exists, without resorting to such drastic measures.

Then again, such a course of action may not be feasible. The scientists may merely dismiss any and all videos out of hand.

It is possible the animal comes out of the water on occasion, and if that is the case, it may be possible to obtain some DNA. I cannot think of any reason the animal would come out of the water, but that does not mean it does not happen.

This is not to say that a combination of videos and DNA would necessarily persuade the scientists of the existence of this animal, as they are determined that it went extinct many millions of years ago.

This brings us back to the one sure fire way to prove the animal exists, the" old school" method of shooting an animal to prove the species exists. If the scientists persist in being completely pig headed, we may have to resort to such a drastic method. A carcass of the animal will certainly get their attention.

I suspect there is no other way to prove the existence of the ichthyosaur.

26

CORONA VIRUS AND STATISTICS

The daily death toll in America, as a result of the corona virus, has just reached a record 502, so that nearly 3,000 Americans have now died, as a result of the sickness. That number is expected to rise dramatically, as the virus continues to spread. The medical experts are predicting an eventual death toll of between 100,00 and 200,000, although others predict the death toll could rise to the millions. To support their predictions, the medical experts are producing graphs, charts and" curves which must be flattened"," epicenters"," hot spots" and percentages, number of people infected and number of fatalities.

Perhaps the medical professionals and journalists are convinced that most common people, members of the public, are at heart mathematically inclined, as it is only mathematicians who find these figures and charts to be fascinating. Such is hardly the case. Or perhaps those same people are of the opinion that it is necessary to confuse common people, as they do not want anyone to understand the breadth and depth of their incompetence.

With that in mind, it is best to explain a few simple terms, which many people may find to be a bore, but bear with me, as this is important. The medical people love to speak in terms of percentages, so let us start with that.

Think of a base of one hundred people, so that one person is one out of a hundred, referred to as one percent. For every one hundred people who get the virus and one person dies, then the fatality rate, which is the death rate, is one percent. By contrast, if five of those hundred people die as a result of getting the virus, then the fatality rate is five percent.

That is quite simple, but then the fatality rate can be expressed in different terms, such as four-point two percent, or 4.2%. Think of this as 42 out of 1,000, or forty-two people out of one thousand people who are infected, and destined to die.

Now the press is reporting that worldwide, there are 775,300 people who are infected with the corona virus. Of those people who are infected, 36,900 have died. By dividing the number of people who have died by the number of people who have been infected, we arrive as a fatality rate of 4.7%. This means that for every thousand people who are infected by the virus, forty-seven have died.

By contrast, in America, there are a reported 158,400 cases of corona virus, with a death toll of 2,919. That gives us a mortality rate of 1.8%, or one-point eight percent. This means that for every one thousand Americans who catch the virus, eighteen have died. This is lower than the world wide average, for good reason. The medical care in America is far better than in most parts of the world.

These numbers are important, because the medical professionals use them to estimate the number of people who will get sick and die, as a result of this virus. The virus is very contagious, or" catchie", as is the popular term. So, the experts put their calculators to work and estimate that if ten percent of the population, which is ten of every hundred Americans catch the virus, then thirty-three million Americans will be infected. Further, if one-point eight percent of those who are infected were to die, then 594,000 Americans would die.

Those numbers are far higher than the estimated number of Americans who are expected to die as a result of being infected with the virus. The experts have come up with a number of between 100,000 and 200,000. Clearly, they expect far fewer people to be infected with the virus, and they also expect the medical attention they receive to remain at a very high level.

The fact remains that the more people who become infected, the more people will die. It is also a fact that the higher the level of medical care patients receive, the less people will die.

The best we can say about these numbers is that they are wildly optimistic. Perhaps the only way to control the spread of the virus is to isolate people who are infected, to keep them away from other people. They simply cannot infect people with whom they have no contact. This approach has proven effective in other parts of the world.

Compare this with the situation in America. New York City is now considered the" epicenter" of the epidemic in the country. Of the nearly 3,000 dead so far, nearly half have died in the state of New York. On one day alone, 253 people have died in the state. Across the country, the death toll for the day stands at 502. The hospitals in New York City are being described as" swamped", a" medical war zone", with the medical facilities on the verge of collapse. Of the New York City police, thirteen percent are out sick, mainly as a result of being infected with the virus, in the performance of their duties.

The New York City first responders and medical workers are on the" front lines" of this" medical war zone". Many of them are personally shopping for personal protective equipment for themselves and their patients, as there is such a severe shortage. Both hospital staff and first responders are working around the clock, shorthanded and desperate for the proper equipment. It is estimated they will run out of equipment within a week.

The navy hospital ship, the Comfort, has been sent to New York City, in an attempt to take some pressure off the hospitals. In addition, a temporary hospital has been set up in Central Park. It is not clear where they expect to find the equipment or the personnel to work at this hospital.

In addition, those who are classified as working in" essential services", which is to say the delivery personnel, are going on strike, demanding personal protective equipment and hazardous duty pay. Many of these people too are becoming infected with the virus, also in the performance of their duties.

There are numerous other" hot spots" in the country, such as New Orleans, Chicago, Florida, New Jersey and Philadelphia, to name a few. Others are popping up on a daily basis. It is anticipated that the" rural America health care system will be quickly over whelmed". In fact, it is clear that the whole American medical system is in danger of collapse. If that happens, the death rate from the corona virus will sky rocket.

Other countries are taking decisive action. Italy and Spain are completely shut down. People are allowed to leave their homes only to get groceries or in case of an emergency. Only essential services workers are continuing to perform their duties, and they are provided with proper personal protective equipment. The leaders of those countries are aware of the gravity of the situation and are taking the appropriate measures to protect their citizens.

That stands in stark contrast to the American leaders. As Trump stated the issue," We cannot let the cure be worse than the problem itself". As he sees it, the" problem" is the corona virus, and the" cure" is isolation, or" social distancing", to use the technical term. This begs the question: How can isolation be worse than the" problem" of citizens being infected with the virus and many of them dying?

To answer that question, we have only to take a glance at the stock market. This should not be difficult, as the news reports are divided between the devastation caused by the virus, and the dropping stock market. The two are connected, to an extent, as people who are" self-isolating" are not spending their money, if for no other reason than that they do not have any money to spend. A great many people are out of work, and the number is growing, as most small businesses are shutting down. These are considered to be Too Small to Succeed. The major corporations, those which are considered Too Big to Fail, are merely laying off their workers, while receiving massive amounts of corporate welfare.

The contrast is sharp and clear. The country is entering a depression, millions of workers are losing their jobs and will soon lose their houses, to become homeless. Countless people are becoming infected with the virus and many of them will die, if only because the medical treatment they so desperately need is not available. The small business owners, the middle class or petty bourgeois, are being wiped out, forced to join the ranks of the working class, the proletariat. Yet the money they pay in taxes is being given to the super rich, the billionaires, the bourgeoisie! The government cannot afford to equip the medical professionals with the equipment they so desperately need, yet they can afford to donate countless billions to the bourgeoisie!

To add insult to injury, Trump is accusing the medical people of stealing their own equipment! The same people who are putting their lives on the line, risking their health in order to assist those who are sick and injured, are in turn being accused, by their own president, of being thieves! Look who's talking! The" kettle calling the pot black"! Trump is a most accomplished thief, with a long history of stealing at every opportunity. For that reason, he just naturally assumes that everyone else is no different.

I have news for you, Mister President. Not everyone is like you. Working people are poor for a reason. We work for a living! We support ourselves, we contribute to society, we pay taxes, and that is the reason we are poor! You on the other hand are extremely rich, do not pay taxes, do not support yourself, and steal at every opportunity. That is the reason that you, and the other members of your class, the bourgeoisie, are so rich!

What is more, Mister Billionaire President, we have had enough! You and your class, the bourgeoisie, place profits before people! That is the reason you are so reluctant to isolate those who are infected with the corona virus. You are afraid it will cut into your profits! You do not call it profit; you refer to it as the" economy". As if you care about the economy! You care only about your profits!

To put it in popular terms," your days are numbered". The working people are fed up. The essential services workers are now rising up. The nurses are demonstrating, and the delivery service workers are going on strike. This could well be the start of a nationwide protest, a revolutionary uprising. It is just a matter of time, and very likely a short time.

To those who are aware of the revolutionary theories of Marx and Lenin, I can only suggest that you get active and form a proper Communist Party, one which openly advocates for the Dictatorship of the Proletariat. That will help to distinguish yourselves from those who claim to be Marxists, but are revisionists.

As for those who are not aware of those theories, I suggest a careful reading of the Essential Works of Lenin, to start. That should give you a proper grounding in Marxist revolutionary theory. As for those who have little use for theory, may I point out that the success -or failure- of the approaching revolution depends upon the proper application of the theory – or the advice if you will- of Marx and Lenin.

I can also suggest that all working people join the two mainstream political parties, Republican and Democratic, as card carrying members, party bosses. At the moment, they are firmly in the hands of the bourgeoisie. They should be challenged, if for no other reason than to add to the misery of the bourgeoisie. Do not pass up any opportunity to make their lives miserable. Besides, this will provide valuable training for such workers, which will be put to good use after the revolution, after we smash the existing state machinery and crush the bourgeoisie under the Dictatorship of the Proletariat.

The revolution is fast approaching, and is not about to wait until we are prepared. Time is not on our side. Now is the time to act. Spread the advice of Marx and Lenin:

Workers of the World, Unite!
Scientific Socialism!
Dictatorship of the Proletariat!

27

CORONA VIRUS AND THE SURGE

April first today, April Fool's day. As I watch the news, I cannot help but wonder if the politicians and economists are not fabricating some sort of twisted April Fool's day joke. But then I realize that it is merely wishful thinking on my part. That which is happening now is too sick to be a joke, too terrible to be a nightmare. Our leaders are too incompetent, too stunned to face reality.

President Trump has ten thousand ventilators in stock, and he is holding on to them. The hospitals are desperately short of medical supplies, including ventilators, yet Trump is not impressed by this. He is saving them for the next two weeks, when" the surge is coming". He is convinced the corona virus pandemic will peak within the next two weeks. No one knows the reason for this belief, but then Trump believes strongly in intuition.

Most of the country is in a state of lockdown, at least until the end of April. After that, he expects the country to" return to normal", in time for fall and the elections. It is clear that Trump is living in his own little world, a world of delusion.

It is true that eighty percent of the country is in a state of lockdown, which means that twenty percent of the country is not locked down. Simple math tells us that *66 million* people are running around, spreading the virus. This is not rocket science.

The medical experts are predicting that the death toll from the virus could reach 240,000. Then again, one of the most highly respected medical professionals, Dr. Brix, gave a figure of *two million!* These impressive numbers did not come to the doctors in the form of a sacred vision. Instead, they played with some numbers, did the math, and came to some different conclusions. The reason for the vastly different estimates for the death toll is quite simple. No one has any idea of the number of people who will contract the virus, so we can only work with estimates. Or you can call them guesses if you like, because that is precisely what they are.

With that in mind, may I suggest that readers apply the same math that the medical experts are using, as it is not difficult, and determine your own estimate. This may help to give the readers some idea of the magnitude of the problem.

The population of the country is roughly three hundred thirty million, or 330,000,000, to put it in mathematical form. If even five percent - expressed as 5%- of the population contracts the virus, then roughly sixteen million people will be infected. Of those sixteen million people, we can expect possibly two percent, – 2%- of those people to die. Using that estimate, we can expect 320,000 fatalities.

The trouble being that we have no idea of the percentage of the population who will be infected. We do know that the more people move around, the more people will be infected, the higher the percentage of infected people. By contrast, the more people sit tight, the less people will be infected, the lower the percentage of the population who will be infected. Hence, the estimate of the percentage of the people who will be infected can only remain a guess. We also know that the more people who are infected, the more people will die, especially if the medical system in the country breaks down.

Then there are other facts, which are awkward, as well as not pleasant. The fact is that in the last three days, the fatality rate, as a result of the virus, has doubled to 835, and that was the death rate in one day. We now have 4,564 total dead, and that number is rising. New York City has been hit very hard, and is considered to be the" epicenter" of the pandemic in America, possibly because so many people are forced to live so close together. Within that city, seventeen percent of the police are out sick, mainly as a result of contracting the virus, in the performance of their duties.

Other" hot spots" include New Jersey, New Orleans, Florida, Detroit, Albany, Texas, Philadelphia, California, Miami and Georgia. Medical supplies are in demand, including personal protective equipment, such as masks, and those which are available are selling *for ten to twenty times the usual price!* Here we have a bright shining example of capitalism in all its glory. The corona virus is ravaging the country, countless people are sick and many are dying, first responders and medical personnel are putting their lives on the line, trying to help the infected, and the *capitalists are using this as an opportunity to enrich themselves!*

That brings us to the economists for the largest, most highly respected financial institutions in the country. They are predicting this little downturn in the economy, this" recession", will turn around" by the fourth quarter". They must live in the same fantasy world as Trump.

Someone should advise these mental midgets that there are -or were- thirty million small businesses in the country. These small businesses employed nearly half the private work force. Very few of those businesses can afford to remain idle for more than a week or two. Now they are faced with the prospect of being idle for six to eighteen months! Few, if any, can afford to shut down for that long. It follows that most, if not all, of their work force is about to be unemployed. Most of the owners are also about to join the ranks of the working class, also unemployed. In short, the unemployment rate is sky rocketing. As that is the case, Mister Big Business Economist, just where do you get the idea that the economy is about to boom once again, later on in the year? Feel free to get it through that thick skull of yours that the country is now entering a depression, one that is expected to be more severe than the one of the nineteen thirties.

But then, as Lenin pointed out, it is the task of the bourgeois economist to" present it in a favorable light". He goes on to say that" simplicity of mind on the part of the bourgeois economists is not surprising. Besides, *it is in their interests* to pretend to be so naive". (italics by Lenin) It is safe to say that the bourgeois economists are certainly earning their pay!

The biggest businesses, the monopoly corporations, those which are referred to as Too Big to Fail, are now even bigger, more powerful, wealthier than ever before, if only because of the government handouts, the corporate welfare, in the guise of the Economic Stimulus Package. The class of people who own those corporations, the billionaires who are technically referred to as the bourgeoisie, are now far wealthier. At the same time, the small business owners, the petty bourgeois, are effectively wiped out. They are being forced into the ranks of the working class, the proletariat. The monopolies are becoming ever stronger, ever more complete. It is to their advantage as they now have no competition from the small business owners, the middle class, the petty bourgeois.

Many of those former members of the middle class, petty bourgeois, are aware of the revolutionary theories of Marx and Lenin. They used to live a relatively comfortable life as small business owner. Those days are gone, never to return. Now they are being forced into the ranks of the working class, the proletariat. To such people, I have only one word: Welcome!

Now may I suggest that you share your class awareness with the other members of the class you have just joined. Explain to workers the existence of classes and the necessity of revolution and the subsequent Dictatorship of the Proletariat. Put your organizational skills to work in preparing demonstrations and marches. Harass the bourgeoisie, allow them no rest. Give them no peace. Encourage all Americans to join the Republican Party and the Democratic Party. Form a most exclusive Communist Party, one which advocates the Dictatorship of the Proletariat. The working class needs leaders.

I will end this article with my usual slogans, as they are so important:

Workers of the World, Unite!
Scientific Socialism!
Dictatorship of the Proletariat!

28

TO THE -FORMER- SMALL BUSINESS OWNERS

The United Nations has now referred to the Corona Virus as" the most challenging issue the world has faced since World War 2". It has spread around the world, with the number of reported cases now over one million, with 54,000 fatalities. America is the country with the most reported cases of the virus, with almost a quarter million infected and 6,000 dead. The American health care system is in danger of being overwhelmed.

The medical professionals anticipate running out of equipment within a few days. Hospitals in all fifty states are being forced to" bid against each other", in an attempt to buy the medical equipment, they so desperately need. This includes not only ventilators, but also personal protective equipment, such as face masks, so as to give the staff a measure of protection from the virus. As the situation becomes ever more desperate, the price of all such medical equipment continues to rise.

The capitalists refer to this as the "law of supply and demand". The greater the demand, the higher the price of the items which are available, so they do their best to limit the supply, possibly hoarding such things as face masks, in order to increase profits. As a result of this, the fact is that countless people are getting sick and many of them are dying. This is of no concern to the capitalists. They are only concerned with their profit, their "bottom line". This pandemic, which is sweeping the world and causing untold suffering, they see as an "opportunity". Make no mistake, they are taking full advantage of this "opportunity", making money "hand over fist".

New York City is currently considered to be the "epicentre" of the outbreak in America, with the hospitals and medical staff stretched to the limit. The New York Fire Department, as "first responders", is reported to have 3,000 members out sick, mainly as a result of being exposed to the virus, in the performance of their duties. In addition, the president of the New York Nurses Association pointed out that "it does not matter how many ventilators we have, if we are dead". That girl has a way with words!

The American military is not indifferent to the suffering of the citizens, and has graciously sent a military hospital ship, the Comfort, to New York City, to help relieve the pressure. The only stipulation is that the ship will only allow patients who are *not* infected with the virus to be treated. In that way, hospital beds in the city will become available for those who are infected with the virus.

The patients who are identified as candidates for transferral to the Comfort must first be tested, to see if they have the virus. It takes several days to get the test results, and most hospital patients are released after four or five days. So by the time the test results are produced, the patients are usually released.

As a result of this, the Comfort, which has a thousand beds and has been docked in New York harbour for three days, has possibly twenty patients. The medical staff within the city do not refer to this ship as the Comfort. They refer to it as the "Floating Joke".

The press reports that certain hospitals are filled to capacity and even overflowing, with patients being placed in hall ways. The doctors are referring to the situation as a "medical war zone". There is a palpable sense of despair and frustration within the medical community. The medical crisis is expected to intensify, as the infection rate has not yet reached a "peak", to use the popular term. It is just a matter of time, and probably a short time, before the health care system in the country is overwhelmed. Even now, there are people who are infected and very sick, yet refuse to go to the hospital. They choose to remain at home and die surrounded by their families, as opposed to going to the hospital and dying alone. The sad fact is that people who are placed on ventilators have only a twenty percent chance of recovering. This means that of every five people placed on ventilators, only one is likely to survive. The other four can be expected to survive for days or even weeks, on "life support", but almost certainly die once the machine is removed.

This is *not* to say that patients should be denied ventilators, or anything else they need. It is to say that many of the ventilators which the federal government has in storage are in need of repair. The mayor of New York City is of the opinion that the federal government should "step up" and provide more assistance, before more people die needlessly. As the highest single day increase in deaths and hospitalizations has just been reported, there is no time to lose.

As the "federal government" to which he is referring is led by President Trump, no less, this "assistance" is not about to take place. There are still ten states which have no "stay at home" rules, so the folks in those states are continuing to travel and gather, to their hearts content, and spread the corona virus. These states are considered to be "rural", sparsely populated, so that the health care system in such areas are not on a par with that which is available in "urban" centres. It is anticipated that any outbreak of the virus will quickly overwhelm the few hospitals which are available.

For that matter, it is just a matter of time before the medical system all across the country breaks down. In other parts of the world, there are reports of victims of the virus dropping dead in the streets, as the hospitals are filled to capacity. Now the press is starting to face reality and reporting that the virus is anticipated to be with us for months and not weeks. After that, it is the opinion of medical experts that we could then be faced with a "second wave". Possibly they anticipate that the virus could "mutate", and return with a vengeance.

It is worth noting that world wide, the death rate for those infected with the virus is roughly five percent, while in America the death rate is around half, at perhaps two point five percent. The medical care in the country is clearly superior to other parts of the world, and those who are kept alive on ventilators, if only for a few days, are not classified as fatalities. That helps to keep the fatality rate at an artificially low level. As the medical system in the country becomes ever more overburdened, we can expect that number to grow.

In the midst of all this devastation, President Trump has a well established set of priorities. He has called up the leaders of Russia and Saudi Arabia and expressed his concern over the price of oil! He wants them to limit their production of oil, as the low price of oil is adversely affecting the stock market. *Americans are getting sick and dying, and Trump is worried about the price of oil!* It is strange, but perhaps not too surprising, that the Kremlin is not aware of this call!

The medical professionals, the "first responders" and the delivery workers, those who are providing desperately needed equipment to those who are in need, in turn need our support. They are risking their health and even their lives, in order to assist those who so desperately require help. To such people I can only offer my most sincere thanks.

With that in mind, and considering the fact that we are now entering a depression, may I suggest that it is high time people take action. The internet and modern communications, by which I mean various digital devices, have provided us with valuable tools. We would be fools to not take advantage of them. We are not our grandparents, we are more aware now than they ever were, and we should act accordingly.

Recently, the American women and students have proven themselves to be excellent organizers. They have managed to arrange protests across the country. Those protests were mainly focused on Trump and gun violence. Now it is once again necessary to protest, the difference being that this time such protests must not be limited to one issue. People must "broaden their horizons", and focus on destroying the whole system of capitalism.

As for those who find that somewhat unreasonable, feel free to face the facts. The country is entering a depression, even broader and deeper than the Great Depression. The country is "head over heels" in debt, and cannot possibly come out of it. Equally without doubt, the capitalists fully intend to try, possibly by provoking a war with Iran. Millions of working people, proletarians, are now losing their jobs. As well, millions more small business owners, middle class people, petty bourgeois, are losing their businesses, facing bankruptcy. They too are unemployed. All are about to also lose their medical coverage and their homes. Many will be forced to live in their cars and even under bridges. As Sargent Friday of Dragnet fame was fond of saying, these are "just the facts".

It is also a fact that there are over 600 billionaires in the country, and they are *profiting from this depression!* The "Economic Stimulus Package", otherwise known as "Corporate Welfare", has served to enrich them. The federal government has chosen to bless those chosen few, those who own businesses which are Too Big To Fail, with vast sums of money, hundreds of billions. This money was collected from American taxpayers, those who are Too Small To Succeed. Bear in mind that these Sacred Six Hundred are members of a class which are technically referred to as the bourgeoisie. They run the country, and are only concerned with "lining their own pockets". They can and must be destroyed.

With that in mind, may I suggest that the "army" of women and students has just received "reinforcements", in the form of those who have recently been ruined by the bourgeoisie. Of course, I am referring to the former small business owners, newly created proletarians. No doubt many of them are quite bitter -who can blame them?- as their dreams of becoming successful and even of joining the ranks of the bourgeoisie, have been completely crushed. Practically overnight, their life savings, their years of hard work, have been flushed down the toilet.

Those same people are now being offered small business loans. To accept those loans would only prolong the agony, driving those people ever deeper into debt. This is a depression, and in a depression, there is no room for any small business. Further, there is no way out of this crisis in capitalism. Face the fact that your businesses are gone and not coming back.

Now is the time to cast away the dreams of success, to transform that bitterness into determination, to face the fact that capitalism has had its day, that revolution and socialism is on the horizon. The world will be a far better place without capitalism!

Join the ranks of the women and students, those who have marched for change, in the past. As formerly successful business people, you have valuable knowledge and skills, which can be of great service to the working class. Most of you are aware of the revolutionary theories of Marx and Lenin, especially that of the necessity of scientific socialism, which includes the smashing of the existing state machinery and establishing the Dictatorship of the Proletariat. Feel free to bring this awareness to the working class. You can speak from experience, so working people are more likely to listen to you.

Time is not on our side, as the revolution waits for no one. It will break out when it breaks out. People are bound to rise up spontaneously, and are in desperate need of class consciousness. That is where middle class, conscious people can be of great service. As it is my most fervent belief that the best way to reach the vast majority of people is with slogans, may I suggest:

Workers of the World, Unite!
Scientific Socialism!
Dictatorship of the Proletariat!

29

AMERICA EDGING CLOSER TO DISSOLVING

The country is entering the Second Great Depression, that which is expected to be even more severe than the Great Depression of the early twentieth century. The hardship is compounded by the pandemic of the corona virus, so that people are referring to this as a "double whammy". In desperation, people are looking for leaders. They are appealing to their democratically elected leader, and in particular the president of the United States, Donald Trump. He takes no responsibility for the crisis which is sweeping the country.

One writer in particular, a true starry eyed optimist, stated that Trump is facing a "problem that can't be solved with his usual bag of political tools, obfuscation, denial, deflecting blame and misinformation". If only that were true!

In fact, Trump denies ever having met with medical professionals in January, in which he was warned of the danger of the corona virus. He was advised of the necessity of containing the virus, of isolating infected areas as well as the individuals who are infected, of preparing for the out break of the anticipated pandemic, of stocking up on medical supplies and giving people warning. This he denies, just as he denies clearly stating, on February 25, "We are very close to a vaccine". In fact, the medical professionals are convinced that such a vaccine is at least a year away.

He also stated, on February 28, "Its going to disappear one day, its like a miracle, it will disappear, it will go away." He went on to speculate that "warm weather will kill the virus", despite the fact that there is nothing to suggest that the weather will have any effect on the virus. Then on March 7, he said that "anyone who wants a test for the virus can get one". Such is hardly the case, as to this day, such a test is not widely available.

As Trump recently stated, he "takes no responsibility for this virus". The lack of preparation, the "empty shelves", he has nailed on the previous administration. The fact that he has been in office for over three years is conveniently overlooked. The journalists who point this out to him, in turn face his wrath and scorn. This is especially true if that journalist is a female. Trump has little patience for women who do not "know their place"!

This brings us to his top political adviser, his son in law, Jared Kushner. He occupies a "special post" inside the Federal Emergency Management Agency. The duties of this "special post" are carefully not specified. Those who work inside the White House refer to him as the leader of the "Slim Suit Crowd".

What ever his official duties may or may not be, we are grateful to Kushner for clarifying the position of the Trump administration, concerning their attitude towards the individual states. As Kushner stated so clearly -if not eloquently- "The notion of the federal stockpile was, it's supposed to be our stockpile. It's not supposed to be the states stockpiles, that they then use."

There we have it, folks. Jared Kushner has just drawn a clear distinction *between "us", or the "federal', and "they", or the individual states!* The individual states which comprise the United States are of no consequence! The "stockpiles" of the "federal" are not to be used by the states! The United States are no longer "United", merely a miscellaneous assortment of individual states which cannot "use" the "federal stockpile"!

To think that most Americans were of the impression that America, by which they meant the United States, was just that! A group of states which were united in purpose, brought together under one federal government, a single country. Such is hardly the case, at least according to Jared Kushner.

It is very likely that the "us" to whom Kushner refers, is nothing other than himself, his father in law, Donald Trump, and the other billionaires in the country, the Sacred Six Hundred, the super rich, the members of the class of people whom are technically referred to as the bourgeoisie. They rule the country, and have donated hundreds, if not thousands, of billions of dollars to the major corporations which they own. These corporations are considered to be "Too Big To Fail", as opposed to the numerous small businesses, which are considered to be Too Small To Succeed. For that matter, countless common people are now losing their jobs, houses and life savings, but we too are Too Small To Succeed. We do not count.

Now the latest absurdity from Trump is that "We see light at the end of the tunnel". Such is hardly the case, for as Dr. Fauci, his top medical adviser put it, "This is going to be a bad week... We are struggling to get it under control". The Surgeon General clearly agrees, as he expects the "week ahead to be the hardest and saddest." He also says "we are facing a crucial two week period...a Pearl Harbour and a nine eleven moment...with a lot of deaths."

As a journalist just reported, precisely a month ago, the death toll from the virus was precisely eleven. Now, one month later, the death toll is *ten thousand!* All this talk of the "peaking of the virus", of "flattening the curve", is just that. Talk. The virus continues to spread, making countless people sick and killing a great many. Further, as thousands of people are desperately sick, kept alive on ventilators, most of those people will soon die, as soon as they are removed from ventilators.

This stands in stark contrast to Trump, the "eternal optimist", who is suggesting the use of an untested drug. As he put it, "What do you have to lose?" In answer to the question, the president of the AMA replied, "You could lose your life."

To this day, ninety six percent of the country is placed on "stay at home orders", or at least forced to exercise "social distancing", so that people leave their homes only when absolutely necessary. In other words, *thirteen million people are still moving around, spreading the virus!* Trump refuses to exercise his executive authority and force the whole country onto "stay at home" orders. As a result of this, ever more "hot spots" continue to appear.

The state of New York has been very hard hit by the virus, with nearly half of the deaths in the country occurring in that one state. Yet when the governor of the state called up the White House and requested more medical equipment, including face masks and ventilators, he was told that he did not know what he had in his own state inventory! Other governors, of other states, have reported similar conversations.

The medical personnel, including first responders as well as hospital staff, are putting their lives as well as their health on the line. In return, they are asking for proper protective gear, such as face masks, as well as hazardous duty pay. In response, the government authorities are telling them "now is not the time". Bear in mind that "now is the time" to bless the biggest, richest, most powerful corporations with mountains of money, tax payer money no less, but the same people who dole out this money have no time to listen to working people!

To all working people, I can only say that now is the time to *act!* We do not have the time to wait for the virus to run its course. By that time, millions of people will be homeless, as well as unemployed. We have to take action now, to march, as the women marched across the country, at the time Trump was inaugurated, three years ago. The students also marched, in protest of gun violence. Now all Americans, of all walks of life, have got to come together, put aside our differences, and *overthrow the system of capitalism, destroy the bourgeois state apparatus and establish the Dictatorship of the Proletariat!*

Now is the time for *scientific socialism!* It is the billionaires, the monopoly capitalists, the bourgeoisie, who are responsible for this disaster. They are using this as an opportunity to line their own pockets! The problem is not one of Trump or

Kushner, but of the class they represent, the bourgeoisie! The whole class must be destroyed! In the process, we can expect the country to break up, as the empire collapses, as working people set up a democratic republic, of the people, by the people and for the people, the working people, the proletariat!

The same people who organized the women's march, as well as the students march, must once again become active and organize once again, only this time with the goal of overthrowing the bourgeoisie. All citizens should be encouraged to join the two mainstream political parties, as card carrying members. All conscious people, those who are familiar with the revolutionary theories of Marx and Lenin, should focus also on forming a proper Communist Party, one which advocates the Dictatorship of the Proletariat. In this way, the Party will be able to distinguish itself from the revisionist parties.

It is to be hoped that this depression and virus will serve as a "wake up call". The people are desperate for leaders. Feel free to rise to the occasion.

30

MEDICAL SYSTEM CLOSE TO COLLAPSE

The single day death toll in the country, as a result of the virus, has reached a record 1,800, bringing the grand total to over 13,000. The virus is decimating the country, causing terrible suffering. The families of those who are dying in hospitals are not allowed to visit them, as the fear is that such visits could lead to more spreading of the virus. As a result of this legitimate concern, such patients are forced to die without being surrounded by family. Further, the family is then forced to arrange a funeral with very few mourners, due to the rules concerning social distancing.

In the midst of this devastation, the journalists are reporting a "glimmer of hope", a "light at the end of the tunnel." They report that the "curve is flattening", that we are "reaching the apex", that the anticipated death toll "may be less than the anticipated 150,000". Perhaps they think the families of the victims of the virus may take some comfort in this!

As soon as someone dies, it is up to the coroner or Medical Examiner to determine the cause of death. The one and only way to determine if the deceased had the virus, is to administer the test for the virus, which can be done, after death. All too often, this is not being done. The test kits *are not available!*

The president of the Wyoming Coroners Association stated that testing procedures for the dead are limited, and doubts that "we will ever know the true impact on fatalities from covid, both for the living and the dead."

The coroner of Arkansas Clark County was somewhat less polite, when he stated, "Bodies aren't tested for covid19. Period."

The coroner in Douglas County, Colorado, has been begging for test kits. As she put it, "If you die in my county, I will not know if you died of covid19."

The coroner in Chester County, Pennsylvania, was a bit more diplomatic when she stated "Testing has been so restricted and test kits so unavailable, I do not think we really know the scope of the infection or virus related deaths here."

Coroners all across the country are expressing a similar frustration.

The simple fact is that no one knows precisely how many people are dying as a result of becoming infected with the virus. For that matter, no one even knows how many people are becoming infected with the virus! The hospitals are filled to capacity and beyond, with patients being placed in the hallways. Many people who are sick are being turned away from the hospital, if only because they appear to *not* be in a life threatening state. There is no time or place for such people. Such patients frequently die at home.

This helps to explain the "flattening of the curve", the "apex of the virus", the reason fewer people are dying than was anticipated. The infection and death of a great many people *is not being reported!*

This frustration is shared by the medical workers, the first responders and the delivery service workers. The medical system is at the point of collapse. In one case, two nurses were expected to care for twenty six patients, ten of whom were on ventilators. It is absolutely not reasonable to expect two nurses to provide quality care for patients, under those circumstances. Such examples are by no means isolated incidents. They are common place.

Recently in Detroit, the night shift emergency nursing staff refused to work and demanded more nurses be brought into their overrun emergency room. The hospital administrators in turn told those nurses to either go to work, or go home. A few of them did go home, and the day shift nurses were ordered to continue working, *for a twenty four hour shift!*

The head of the Michigan Nurses Association spoke quite clearly when she said "A tipping point is reached where the best thing any RN can do for their patients, their families and their coworkers is to speak out rather than remain silent...it is only a matter of time before more actions like this occur. It is absolutely essential that hospitals start working with nurses and stop silencing our voices."

In this she is absolutely right, in so far as "speaking out" is the "best thing any RN can do". On the other hand, there is no way the hospital administrators are about to listen to the nurses, nor are they about to "stop silencing" their voices. The hospital staff is in the service of the class of people who run the country, the capitalists, the billionaires, the Sacred Six Hundred, the bourgeoisie. These people are imperialists, and as Lenin put it, "Imperialism is reaction, right down the line". As that is the case, we can expect nothing progressive from these people.

Some of the delivery workers, those who supply the hospitals with medical supplies and are classified as essential services, are already on strike. Any day now, the hospital staff will join them, as they reach the "tipping point", the point where people cannot take any more, where they say "enough is enough". They are risking their health and even their lives, without proper protective clothing to wear, a shortage of medical equipment, over worked so that they simply cannot perform a proper job, and disrespected by the hospital administrators. There are limits.

This anticipated strike action, on the part of the medical workers, could well be the beginning of a full scale revolution. It is not just the medical system that is at the stage of crisis, set to collapse. The whole system of capitalism is in crisis, although it is doubtful that the capitalists are aware of this. Even if they are aware, they are not about to acknowledge this. As that is the case, perhaps we should draw it to their attention. It is the least we can do. We owe them so much, and it is high time we got even!

The virus has spread around the world, and this is just the start of the Second Great Depression. Even after the virus has run its course, or at least the first wave of the virus, the depression will remain.

It is to be hoped that the current situation will serve as a "call to arms", that conscious people, those who are aware of the revolutionary theories of Marx and Lenin, will come together and form a revolutionary Communist Party, Dictatorship of the Proletariat. It is also hoped that all Americans will put aside their differences and join the two mainstream political parties. As well, the leaders of the Women's March and the Student Protest Movement should once again stage massive protests, this time in support of our heroic medical professionals and against the system of capitalism. They have done it before and they can do it again.

As for the groups who are determined to force through paltry reforms, feel free to face the fact that such reforms are not about to take place. It is time for people of all backgrounds to come together, regardless of race, religion, creed, belief or class heritage. Bear in mind that Marx and Lenin were middle class intellectuals. It is such people who are obligated to bring the class awareness to the working class, the proletariat. *Intellectuals are not to be scorned!*

On the contrary, it is up to workers, or at least the most advanced members of the working class, to raise their level of awareness to *that of the level of intellectuals!* Feel free to earn the mantle of working class intellectual! The revolutionary writings of Marx and Lenin are readily available, as is the internet. Make use of these tools, as it is in your best interest.

I most passionately hope that Americans will once again become active, as they have in the past. After all, they have a revolutionary history, of which they can be most proud. March with banners, this time proclaiming class content, calling for scientific socialism, an end to capitalism, the defeat of the billionaires, the Sacred Six Hundred, the bourgeoisie. The beginning of the Dictatorship of the Proletariat.

I will close this article with suggestions for my usual slogans, as it gives people a place to start:

Workers of the World, Unite!
Scientific Socialism!
Dictatorship of the Proletariat!

31

REVOLUTION IN INDUSTRIALIZED COUNTRIES

Capitalism has just given rise to no less than two crises, which are happening at the same time. The corona virus is sweeping the world, leaving death and devastation in its wake. At the same time, the capitalist world is now entering a Second Great Depression. More death and destruction!

As Lenin pointed out in Imperialism, the Highest Stage of Capitalism, "Crises of every kind -economic crises more frequently, but not only these- in their turn increase very considerably the tendency towards concentration and monopoly."

The twin crises we are currently experiencing are providing us with very clear cut examples of this. In the last three weeks alone, an estimated *17 million workers* filed for unemployment insurance benefits. Countless small businesses are shut down, the vast majority of which will never reopen. Even after the country recovers from the effects of the corona virus, the depression will continue. The major businesses, the monopolies, the "chains" of super markets, airlines, railroads, hotels, mines and mills, for example, are open for business now and will continue to remain open. The only difference is that now, they do not have any competition from the small business owners. The monopolies are now stronger, more complete. Those whom the capitalists have deemed "Too Big To Fail" will thrive, while the rest of us, those who are Too Small To Succeed, will go the way of the dodo bird.

This is to the advantage of the monopoly capitalists, the billionaires, the Sacred Six Hundred, the bourgeoisie. They own these corporations, and have already given themselves *trillions of dollars* of tax payer money. For the benefit of those who are not aware, I will point out that a trillion is a *thousand billion!* The crisis continues to intensify. The small business owners, the middle class, the petty bourgeois is being wiped out. As Lenin put it, "it is the petty bourgeois that every war and every crisis ruins and destroys first". Yet they are not the only ones who are facing ruin.

Millions of workers, proletarians, are losing their jobs, soon to lose their houses and everything else they own, including their life sayings, forced into bankruptcy. And the bourgeoisie? They are rolling in wealth! They have never been richer. Those who used to have billions now have tens of billions! This is truly "the best of times, the worst of times".

This is another way of saying that the situation is revolutionary. The suffering of the common people, the members of the public, is severe and about to become ever more intense. The capitalists expect us to suffer through this depression, much as our grand parents suffered through the first great depression. Possibly they are not aware that we are not our grandparents. We are far more aware than they ever were. We are not about to put up with the this crap, as our grandparents did. Perhaps we should let them know this!

The internet, movies and popular television shows have helped to educate the members of the public. Now it is up to conscious people, Marxists, to further educate the working class, to raise their level of awareness, to explain to people the existence of classes, of the necessity of revolution and the subsequent Dictatorship of the Proletariat. We currently live under the dictatorship of the bourgeoisie. The capitalists are in charge and fully intend to remain in charge. The only alternative is the Dictatorship of the Proletariat. As we live in a class society, there is no third alternative.

We can learn from the Russian revolution, as it was similar to the current situation, but there were also important differences. Three quarters of the Russian population was composed of peasants, most of whom had no education. As most of the country was not highly industrialized, it was different from the current American situation. As Lenin put it, "In such a country it was quite easy to start a revolution". On the other hand, in such a country, carrying through the revolution is exceptionally difficult. Or as Lenin phrased it, "it was easy for the Russian revolution to begin but difficult for it to take further steps."

Lenin went on to compare the Russian revolution to that of highly industrialized countries, within Europe. "The European revolution will have to begin against the bourgeoisie, against a much more serious enemy and under immeasurably more difficult conditions. It will be much more difficult for the European revolution to begin. We see that it is immeasurably more difficult to make the first breach in the system that is holding back the revolution. It will be much easier for the European revolution to advance to the second and third stages." That is because "the degree of organization and solidarity of the proletariat there is incomparably greater." He went on to say that "It is more difficult to start a revolution in West European countries because there the revolutionary proletariat is opposed by the higher thinking that comes with culture, and the working class is in a state of cultural slavery."

That which applies to Western Europe also applies to America, but with an additional difference. In respect to America, there is one more detail which has to be taken into account. As Lenin also stated, "The trade unions have never embraced more than one fifth of the wage workers in capitalist society, even under the most favourable circumstances, even in the most advanced countries... only a small upper stratum were members, and of them a very few were lured over and bribed by the capitalists to take their place in capitalist society as workers leaders. The American socialists called these people 'labour lieutenants of the capitalist class....who were bribed and bought by it.'"

The point is that there are members of the working class, within America, who are quite well paid, "bribed" by the capitalists, those who may or may not be union leaders, but quite content to serve their masters, the capitalists. To these "labour lieutenants of the capitalist class", may I suggest that you "mend your ways". You are probably not aware of the fact that you are about to become a target of the revolution. Feel free to "convert", as otherwise the experience of the revolution will make you wish you had. If there is one thing we find more contemptible than the capitalists, it is their belly crawling boot lickers.

Now to the American women, my female comrades, I can only say that you have proven yourselves to be excellent organizers. That is fine, as far as it goes, but it does not go far enough. Those of you who are not aware of the revolutionary theories of Marx and Lenin have to "brush up", to educate yourselves. Those of you who are aware of the revolutionary theories have to put it into practice. Face the fact that capitalism has had its day, it is in its death throes. There is no way out of this crisis, this depression. The world will never again be the same.

Now is the time to step up, to distinguish yourselves as revolutionary leaders, to follow in the footsteps of Rosa Luxembourg. She was a fine revolutionary, one who devoted her life to the cause of revolution. She refused to compromise her principles, never became a revisionist, never betrayed the working people. It was for that reason that she paid the ultimate price, was murdered by the reactionaries. May her sacrifice be an inspiration to women around the world!

To American men, my comrades, may I offer similar advice. Now is no time to march for paltry reforms -not that it ever was- but to march for the revolution, to overthrow the capitalists, the bourgeoisie. Join your women folk, protect them, prepare to do battle. They call us "rednecks", so embrace the term. Wear red kerchiefs, perhaps over your nose and mouth, to prevent the spread of the virus. Do not allow fear of the virus to divert you from the greater enemy, the bourgeoisie. March to destroy capitalism. March for your women and children. March for scientific socialism. March for the Dictatorship of the Proletariat!

32

NOW WHAT TO DO?

The world of capitalism is being rocked by twin crises. The corona virus is sweeping the world, causing wide spread sickness and death. The most highly developed countries have responded by declaring a state of emergency, closing their borders, placing their citizens under a "lockdown", in that most people are not allowed to leave their homes, unless it is for an emergency or to buy groceries. Even then, all must practice "social distancing", keeping a respectful distance from others. Only "essential personnel" are allowed to keep working, such as hospital staff and "first responders". The idea is to contain the spread of the virus. The effectiveness of this policy varies from one country to another.

The countries which recognized the threat of the virus and immediately took steps to contain it, suffered the least amount of sickness and death. By contrast, the most highly industrialized countries were slow to respond to the crisis caused by the virus. The capitalists who are in charge of such countries were most reluctant to place their countries in "lockdown mode", as that is "bad for business", or as they are so fond of saying, "harms the economy". By that they mean their profits will suffer.

Naturally, of all countries, America was perhaps the slowest to respond. So now they are paying the price, with a half million people who have been confirmed to be infected with the virus, and twenty thousand dead. The vast majority of these fatalities have been seniors.

In addition, all capitalist countries are now entering a depression, although most bourgeois economists are denying this. As Lenin put it, "it is in their interest to do so". Such economists come out with glowing predictions, which are far removed from reality. The alternative is to tell the stock holders the facts, in which case their bosses, the corporate directors, will find some one who is more agreeable. The European Union is on the verge of collapse. None of the bourgeois economists are prepared to admit this, just as they deny that numerous countries are facing bankruptcy. Denial is the "order of the day".

A similar situation existed towards the end of the First World War, in that the most industrialized countries were in a state of crisis. As Lenin put it, "Europe's greatest misfortune and danger is that it has *no* revolutionary party. It has parties of traitors...and servile souls... But it has no revolutionary party." (italics by Lenin) He goes on to say that "a mighty, popular revolutionary movement may rectify this deficiency, but it is nevertheless a serious misfortune and a grave danger."

At that time, the Marxists of the day fully expected the Russian revolution to spread to other countries of the world. May I suggest that one reason it did not, is that the "grave danger", the lack of a "revolutionary party", was at least partly responsible for this. May I also suggest that we suffer from a similar "misfortune", and not just in Europe.

The fact is that people need leaders. This is especially true of the working class, the proletariat, as members of that class are not aware of themselves as a class. This gives the capitalists, the billionaires, the bourgeoisie, a huge advantage. It is the duty of conscious people, Marxists, to bring this awareness to the working class. Further, the most advanced members of the working class must be raised to the level of Marxists.

This is a "tall order", but no where near as difficult as it used to be. The breakthrough in modern communications, that which I refer to as the internet -for lack of a better word- has given the working class a powerful tool. The members of the public are far better educated now than ever before. In particular, various popular television shows have exposed the inner workings of the political system. True, these are works of fiction, but based on fact. The writers of those shows know precisely what they are doing. We are grateful to them.

No doubt there are a great many working class people who are now politically active, as a result of the revolutionary motion. I write this article with those people in mind. Welcome, my brothers and sisters, my comrades!

It is very likely that most working class people are somewhat confused by the people on the Left, by which I mean those who claim to be socialists, independent socialists, Marxist-Leninists or Communists, among other things. But then it is confusing. Which is not to say that the "revolutionary" theories they spout is new and original, because it is not. It is merely a rehash of the same old garbage which was blurted out many years ago, and Lenin had a few choice words for those who endorsed this revisionist nonsense.

During the time that Lenin worked, that which we refer to as Marxism or Communism was referred to as Social Democracy, as it was considered that those who strive for socialism also strive for democracy. That is quite clear and simple, yet there is nothing so simple that bourgeois intellectuals cannot complicate. Social Democracy is no exception.

At that time, a number of bourgeois intellectuals, those who claimed to be Marxists, but were in fact revisionists, which is to say that they were determined to revise the revolutionary theories of Marx, distinguished themselves by coming to the fore front of the revolutionary movement which was then sweeping the country. A similar situation is taking place today. Lenin had a few words for these imposters, those who claim to be Marxists, but are not. As that is the case, perhaps it is best to check in on the lad.

In fact, Lenin wrote What Is To Be Done? with those frauds in mind. As it is so important, I have decided to quote it at some length. The revisionists were of the opinion that "Social Democracy must change from a party of the social revolution into a democratic party of social reforms...The possibility of putting socialism on a scientific basis and of proving that it is necessary and inevitable from the point of view of the materialist conception of history was denied, as also were the facts of growing impoverishment and proletarianization and the intensification of capitalist contradictions. The very conception, *'ultimate aim'* was declared to be unsound, and the idea of the Dictatorship of the Proletariat was absolutely rejected. It was denied that there is any difference in principle between liberalism and socialism. *The theory of the class struggle* was rejected on the grounds that it could not be applied to a strictly democratic society, governed according to the will of the majority, etc...Thus, the demand for a definite change from revolutionary Social Democracy to bourgeois social reformism was accompanied by a no less definite turn towards bourgeois criticism of all the fundamental ideas of Marxism" (italics by Lenin)

Lenin went on to say that this "trend" in Social Democracy is nothing else than a "new species of *opportunism*". (italics by Lenin) For those who are new to the revolutionary movement, I should explain that the word means unprincipled. Further, it has been my experience that those who strive to revise the theories of Marx tend to be completely devoid of principle.

Today few people can deny the "growing impoverishment and proletarianization and the intensification of capitalist contradictions". Certainly the millions of workers who are being laid off can testify to that! In addition to their jobs, they are about to lose their life savings, their houses, cars and everything else they have worked all their lives to attain.

By the same token, the small business owners, the middle class people, the petty bourgeois, are equally well aware of the fact of "proletarianization", as they are being ruined by this crisis in capitalism. Their businesses are closed, never to reopen. They have been forced into the ranks of the proletariat.

As for the "intensification of capitalist contradictions", it is clear for all to see that the capitalists, the billionaires, the bourgeoisie, are thriving! Now more so than ever, they are indeed living in the "lap of luxury". Countless people are sick and dying, so the price of medical equipment has gone through the roof! Simple face masks are now selling for *ten to twenty times* the usual price! Medical personnel and first responders, those who are placing their health and even their lives on the line, are being *gouged!*

Not only are the capitalists reaping "windfall profits" as a result of the virus, they are also stealing countless *billions of tax payer dollars* and giving it to themselves and the corporations which they own. They justify this with the rationale that such corporations are Too Big To Fail. Clearly the rest of us are *Too Small To Succeed!*

It is vitally important that true Communist parties be formed in all the industrialized countries of the world, and not just in Europe. The reason for this is quite simple: *The success of the revolution depends upon this!*

As for those who are skeptical, who think the working class can spontaneously revolt and establish a socialist republic, may I suggest that you could not possibly be more mistaken. As Lenin put it, "Without a revolutionary theory, there can be no revolutionary movement...the importance of theory... is still greater for three reasons...our Party is only in the process of formation, its features are but just becoming outlined, and it has not yet completely settled its accounts with other tendencies in revolutionary thought which threaten to divert the movement from the proper path...what at first sight appears to be an 'unimportant' mistake may give rise to most deplorable consequences... the second reason is that the Social Democratic movement is essentially an international movement…It also means that a movement that is starting in a young country can be successful only on the condition that it assimilates the experience of other countries…The third reason is that the national tasks of Russian Social Democracy are such as have never confronted any other socialist party in the world…the *role of vanguard can be fulfilled only by a party that is guided by an advanced theory.*" (italics by Lenin)

In the same work by Lenin, he went on to quote extensively from Engels. As he put it, "Engels recognized *not two* forms of the great struggle Social Democracy is conducting (political and economic)… *but three, adding to the first two the theoretical struggle.*" (italics by Lenin)

We are now faced with a similar situation, in that the most industrialized countries of the world, including America, are suffering from the "grave danger" and "serious misfortune" of not having a proper Communist Party to give the working class the guidance it so desperately needs. It is absolutely essential that each and every country form its own Communist Party. As for those countries which are cursed with political parties which claim to be Marxist, but are in fact revisionist, may I suggest the name of the party be Communist Party, Dictatorship of the Proletariat, or CP, DP. In this way, the true Marxist parties can be distinguished from the revisionists, as no Marxist revisionist acknowledges the Dictatorship of the Proletariat.

The Communist Party of each country can then focus on raising the level of awareness of the working class, the proletariat. The most advanced workers can be raised to the level of Communists. They in turn will lead the less advanced.

As Lenin pointed out, regardless of the strength of the revolutionary movement, it will not lead to Social Democratic, which is to say Marxist or Communist consciousness. "This consciousness could only be brought to them from without. The history of all countries shows that the working class, exclusively by its own efforts, is able to develop only trade union consciousness...The theory of socialism, however, grew out of the philosophical, historical and economic theories that were elaborated by the educated representatives of the propertied classes, the intellectuals...the founders of modern scientific socialism, Marx and Engels, themselves belonged to the bourgeois intelligentsia."

I should add that this "trade union consciousness", this awareness of the working class, or at least the more advanced members of the working class, that there is "strength in numbers", is as far as the working class can go, by itself. The political revisionist parties which demand only paltry reforms, such as an increase in wages and working conditions, are referred to by Lenin as "Economists". It is characteristic of such people that they "worship" the spontaneous revolutionary movement, and oppose the non-labour "socialist intelligentsia", even though they claim to be members of the socialist intelligentsia! That is a marvel of intellectual gymnastics!

I have no doubt that each country will soon rectify the "grave danger" and "misfortune" of not having a true Communist Party. Just bear in mind that, as Lenin put it, "all subservience to the spontaneity of the labour movement, all belittling of the role of the 'conscious element', of the role of Social Democracy, *means, whether one likes it or not, the growth of influence of bourgeois ideology among the workers.* All those who talk about 'exaggerating the importance of ideology', about exaggerating the importance of the conscious element, etc., imagine that the pure and simple labour movement can work out an independent ideology for itself, if only the workers 'take the fate out of the hands of the leaders'. But this is a profound mistake…Since there can be no talk of an independent ideology being developed by the masses of the workers in the process of their movement, *the only choice is*: either bourgeois or socialist ideology. There is no middle course…to belittle socialist ideology *in any way*, to *deviate from it in the slightest degree* means strengthening bourgeois ideology." (italics by Lenin)

It is my personal opinion that the Russian revolution could not have succeeded without the leadership provided by Lenin. It is further my personal opinion that the revolution did not spread beyond the borders of Russia, because of the "grave danger" and "misfortune" of the lack of a Communist Party in other countries.

No doubt skeptical readers will question why the spontaneous movement, the movement along the line of least resistance, lead to the domination of bourgeois ideology? As Lenin responded, "For the simple reason that bourgeois ideology is far older in origin than Social Democratic ideology; because it is more fully developed and because it possesses *immeasurably* more opportunities for being distributed."

There can be no doubt that the current crisis in capitalism has given birth to a truly revolutionary situation, not just in Europe but also in America. Or especially in America, as the tension is extreme. The revolution could break out any day, but without a Communist Party to provide direction, *it is bound to fail!* The current pack of imbecilic leaders would only be replaced by a new pack of thieves and liars. Capitalism would continue, despite the change of faces.

Under these circumstances, I am convinced that there is nothing more important now than the formation of a Communist Party, in each industrialized country. I consider this to be the "key link" in the chain, as Lenin refers to it. With that in mind, as an answer to my question of Now What To Do?

Create a Communist Party

33

PLATFORM OF AN AMERICAN COMMUNIST PARTY

In my previous article, I mentioned that we are in desperate need of a true Communist Party, one which calls for the Dictatorship of the Proletariat. There are numerous political parties, all of which can legitimately be referred to as "Leftist", and some of whom refer to themselves as Marxist. Each and every one of these parties says something different. As a result of this, the members of the public, the common people, tend to be confused. The best way to draw a clear distinction between the revisionist Communist parties and the true Communist Party is revealed by Lenin in his work, State and Revolution. "A Marxist is one who extends the acceptance of the class struggle to the *Dictatorship of the Proletariat*... This is the touchstone on which the real understanding and acceptance of Marxism should be tested."(italics by Lenin)

The fact is that Marx stated quite clearly that he did not discover the existence of classes, just as he did not discover the struggle between them. These had been discovered by bourgeois historians, and bourgeois economists had described the "economic anatomy of the classes". It is to be stressed that the struggle between the classes is well known and *accepted* by the bourgeoisie. The step forward which Marx did was not acceptable to the bourgeoisie. As Marx put it, "What I did that was new was to prove: 1) that the *existence of classes* is only bound up *with particular historical phases in the existence of production*; 2) that the class struggle necessarily leads to the Dictatorship of the Proletariat; 3) that this dictatorship itself only constitutes the transition to the abolition of all classes and to a classless society."(italics by Lenin)

I have chosen to use capital letters as a means of emphasizing the importance of that dictatorship, rather than italics. So my suggestion is that the name be Communist Party, Dictatorship of the Proletariat, CP,DP.

Without doubt, the Party will have to be formed by intellectuals, most of whom will be current or former members of the middle class, although others could be working class intellectuals. A Party platform will have to be worked out, and I could suggest a platform similar to the original platform of the Russian Social Democratic Labour Party, RSDLP, written by Lenin.

For the sake of those who are new to the revolutionary movement - and I hope there are a great many of you- I will mention that in the year 1898, a handful of middle class revolutionary Russian intellectuals gathered together to form the nucleus of that which came to be known as the Russian Communist Party. The meeting was conducted in great secrecy, as the Czar was completely reactionary and such gathering were strictly forbidden. This did not stop those few people from doing that which had to be done. They put their freedom and even their lives on the line, as a matter of principle. One of those dedicated revolutionaries was Lenin.

He and several others were quickly rounded up, sent to prison and then exiled. A couple others were left free, but only for the purpose of attracting other "subversives".

I mention this as a precaution to all Marxist, those who are interested in forming a true Communist Party. We are not cursed with a Czar, as was Lenin and the early revolutionaries. In fact, Americans are blessed with a Bill of Rights, thanks to the American founding fathers, those who refused to sign the American Constitution, as it did not contain a Bill of Rights. Those men stood on principle, and we owe them a debt of gratitude. Now it is our turn to follow in their footsteps.

With that in mind, I can suggest that reasonable precautions be taken. Just because we have certain democratic rights, as is guaranteed in the Constitution, does not mean that those rights will be respected. A certain circumspection is probably a good idea. Meetings are required, but it is perhaps best not to advertise. Those who are proficient with computers can very likely set up such events on the internet, using skype or some other "social networking" program, assuming that is the proper terms. Even then, various government agencies may well try to eavesdrop. On the other hand, there is a group who call themselves Anonymous, and they are broadcasting with considerable success. Then there is the White House Resistance, which appears to be still on the loose. The federal government has as yet failed to track them down and silence them.

The original platform of the RSDLP, as written by Lenin, is available on the internet, and is no doubt contained in his collected works. Those works are not readily available. However, as we have the internet, feel free to make use of it.

The very important point is that the introduction contains the following clause: "A necessary condition for this social revolution is the Dictatorship of the Proletariat, that is, conquest by the proletariat of such political power as will enable it to suppress any resistance by the exploiters." I consider that to be an absolutely key clause, one which is completely unacceptable to the bourgeoisie. The introduction also calls for the organization of the proletariat into an independent political party, opposed to all the bourgeois parties, a proletarian party which exposes the lies and deception of the bourgeoisie, guides and explains the revolution to the working class.

It also calls for a legislative assembly, a "single chamber". In terms of the American revolution, this means that the Senate should be abolished, in order to make the federal government more democratic. Then there is the call for a "progressive tax" on income, and an inheritance tax. All judges should be elected. I am sure we can all agree on those points.

The new platform of the American Communist Party should also call for the abolition of the Electoral College. All student loans should be declared null and void. Education should be tuition free. There should be an increase to the minimum wage and to pensions. Everyone should be guaranteed free medial care, a human right.

The current situation is becoming ever more tense, ever more revolutionary. The contradictions are becoming ever sharper. The journalists are describing Trump as in the grip of a "melt down". He has produced a propaganda video, at tax payer expense, in which he denies the warnings he received concerning the virus. His lies are becoming ever more blatant.

One journalist even went so far as to use the word "dangerous". This is in a reference to the claim of Trump that he has the "absolute right" to "reopen the country", to open up all states for business. He does not have that right. His power is not absolute. As a result of this, the governors of various states, on each coast, are coming together, forming "coalitions". It is a small step from coalitions to the formation of separate republics, independent from the United States. Such republics could well trigger another civil war, a true revolution.

All of this in no way changes the fact that Americans are among the leaders of the international revolutionary movement. Further, it is American women who are in the forefront of the revolution, if only because the upper stratum of the working class has been bought off by the capitalists. At least, that used to be the case. Now that we are entering a depression, the "perks" those worker used to receive are a thing of the past. As well, the middle class is being devastated. Countless small businesses are closing, with more on the way. It is difficult to see how any small business can survive the depression.

With that in mind, I can suggest that the leaders of the women's movement, many of whom are, or were, members of the middle class, should once again become active. No doubt many of you are aware of the revolutionary theories of Marx and Lenin. Feel free to put those theories into practice. The "good old days" of a comfortable middle class existence are a thing of the past. Now there is a need for a true Communist Party, and it is doubtful that anyone else is prepared to rise to the occasion. I have complete confidence in you.

Only a true Communist Party can bring to the working class, the proletariat, the awareness of themselves as a class, with their own class interests, which are diametrically opposed to the interests of the bourgeoisie. They have to be prepared for the approaching revolution and the subsequent Dictatorship of the Proletariat. There are various ways to raise the level of awareness, so feel free to be creative. So much of the propaganda from various Leftist groups is a supreme bore. People get tired of listening to the same old expressions, so that they tend to lose any meaning. The best way to educate people is to entertain them at the same time. As a bonus, this also irritates the bourgeoisie to no end.

A number of leaders of the women's movement are professional entertainers, and they did some fine work exposing the bourgeoisie in the recent past. Several of these performances were so fine, they appeared on the main stream media. We need more of this, except with more class content. This can be in the form of signs, banners, slogans or even songs. You ladies are talented -do not deny it- so put those talents to good use.

There is a time and a place for protests and demonstrations, and there are other ways to raise the level of awareness of the proletariat. Of course I am referring to the internet. Most members of the public are literate, and now the vast majority have personal computers, or at least have access to them. Certain videos go "viral", if that is the correct word, in that people find them to be quite entertaining. For the most part, this happens more or less by accident. Feel free to produce such videos, hopefully to go viral, but by design.

The American revolution is of particular importance because it will no doubt spread to other countries of the world. Other revolutions in other parts of the world will also spread, so that in the not too distant future, we will see a World Socialist Republic, of which Lenin wrote.

The monopoly capitalists, the bourgeoisie, in the most highly industrialized countries have to be overthrown and crushed under the Dictatorship of the Proletariat. In such countries, it is exceptionally difficult to start the revolution, but once started, it is much easier to proceed. This stands in stark contrast to under developed countries, in that it is relatively easy to start a revolution, but far more difficult to carry it through. The fact that capitalism was restored in Russia as well as China, both under developed countries, is not a coincidence.

Perhaps the ladies who are leading the revolution will take some encouragement from the fact that we can expect a great many more men to take part in the revolution. Those workers who were receiving extra "perks" from the capitalists are now feeling the pinch. A great many middle class people, men as well as women, are now ruined, forced into the ranks of the proletariat. The proletarian army has just increased dramatically in size, becoming far stronger. Now it is no longer quite so difficult to start the revolution, thanks to the bourgeoisie.

This is not to say that we are about to enter the "Age of Aquarius", at a time of "peace and tranquility", because we are not. As anyone who has ever lived through a revolution can testify, it is anything but peaceful. It is on the horizon, it is going to be difficult, it is necessary, and without the proper leadership provided by the Communist Party, it will be a failure.

I have no doubt that conscious people, those who aware of the revolutionary theories of Marx and Lenin, will rise to the occasion and form a true Communist Party. We will know we are on the right track when the expression Dictatorship of the Proletariat is on the lips of all working people.

Forward to the Revolution, my Brothers and Sisters, my Comrades!

34

SEPARATE AMERICAN REPUBLICS FORMING

The fatalities in America, as a result of the corona virus, continue to soar. The reported deaths are currently over thirty six thousand, while the deaths of people who choose to die at home, surrounded by family, are not reported. As well, over twenty two million workers have filed for unemployment benefits *within the last month!* Even that number is expected to "rise dramatically" as those who are currently employed, if only on paper, by various small businesses, are "given their walking papers". The three hundred fifty billion that Congress made available to small businesses has just run out. Without more government hand outs, far more workers will be laid off. As well, the current small business owners, the petty bourgeois, will also be joining the ranks of the proletariat, also unemployed.

This is to say that the country is sinking ever deeper into a depression. The political scientists, the Marxists, may say that the "contradictions are sharpening". I mention this for the benefit of the working people who are reading this article, and I most fervently hope there are a great many such people. All Americans are well aware that the country is deeply divided. Not so many people are aware that it is about to break apart. The country is on the verge of revolution. Separate republics are in the process of formation. The capitalists within those emerging republics are determined to make sure that capitalism persists, even after the revolution.

This could happen. It must be stressed that revolution does not necessarily lead to socialism! During a revolution, people rise up spontaneously, not consciously! I refer to this as an Act of God, while other Marxists, those who may object to the use of the work God, tend to refer to it as a "mass movement". I make no apologies for my belief in God. I respect the beliefs of all others, and merely ask the same respect in turn.

The important point to remember is that the vast majority of people who are about to rise up in the approaching revolution are not "conscious people". No one wakes up one morning and decides to take part in a revolution. Yet that is precisely what happens. That is also the reason we say that such people are acting in a "spontaneous" manner. This is not to denigrate the importance of the spontaneous element. This is to say that the people who are spontaneously taking part in the revolution need to become aware that they are part of a working class, technically referred to as the proletariat. They also have to be made aware of the existence of the capitalist class, the class of parasites opposite to them, the billionaires who make up the class of people referred to as the bourgeoisie. The proletariat and the bourgeoisie are class enemies. In other words, we have to raise the level of awareness of the proletariat. In fact, the most advanced workers must have their level of awareness raised to the level of Marxists.

The most advanced workers are exceptional. Their importance lies in the fact that the vast majority of workers, those whom are somewhat less advanced, pay strict attention to what they say. Advanced workers are well respected. The less advanced workers, those who may scoff at middle class intellectuals, listen closely to the advanced workers.

This is not to say that we, as Marxists, should ignore the less advanced. We want to raise their level of awareness, and the best way to do this is through repetition and the use of slogans. Signs and banners must proclaim the existence of classes, that of workers as well as capitalists. Such terms as scientific socialism and Dictatorship of the Proletariat must become common place. All workers must become aware that it is the Marxist belief that the capitalists must be overthrown and crushed under the Dictatorship of the Proletariat.

Recently, the governors of various states have formed a loose alliance, in that they have agreed to "work together" to "reopen their economies". On the east coast, the states of New York, New Jersey, Connecticut, Pennsylvania, Delaware, Rhode Island and Massachusetts have formed a "coalition". In the midwest, the states of Michigan, Ohio, Wisconsin, Minnesota, Illinois, Indiana and Kentucky have agreed to work in "close cooperation". On the west coast, the states of California, Oregon and Washington have also formed "regional pacts".

These loose "coalitions" or "alliances" or "regional pacts" constitute nothing less than the nucleus of *separate republics* which are forming out of the impending collapse of the American empire. It is Trump who is forcing these states to come together, to form these alliances. He claims to have "total authority". He also stated that the governors who dispute his claim are "engaging in mutiny". As Trump put it, "We have the authority to do whatever we want...will take strong action against states" who dispute this authority. He went on to compare this to the Mutiny On the Bounty.

At that time, the penalty for mutiny was death by hanging. Had the mutineers on board the Bounty been caught, no doubt those people would have faced the death penalty. Equally without doubt, all governors are aware of this. The fact is that Trump has just threatened the governors of all states *with the death penalty*, if they defy his authority!

Of course Trump does not have this legal authority. Under the constitution, there is a clear division of power, between state and federal branches of government. This does not impress Trump in the slightest, as he has all the power he says he has. As far as he is concerned, the constitution is merely a scrap of paper. No wonder the governors of various states are banding together! Their lives are on the line!

No doubt there are numerous people who think that is an exaggeration. They probably think the idea of the Commander in Chief of the American armed forces, sending troops into individual states, with the intent of hanging any and all governors who dare defy him, is madness. As I am not a medical professional, I am not about to argue the mental status of Trump. I will merely point out that Trump "welcomes mutiny", and is prepared to take "strong action" against mutineers. We know this for a fact, because those are precisely the words he used!

As for those who are skeptical, may I draw your attention to a previous head of state, one whom also made some very wild, reckless statements. He threatened to invade neighbouring countries, kill most of the citizens, and enslave the rest. He also threatened to kill a whole race of people, an act of genocide. He was not joking. We know this for a fact, as he went on to do precisely as he threatened. It is not clear why so many people were shocked.

It was Marx who pointed out that in a time of crisis, "the ruling class can no longer rule in the old way. They have to change their method of rule". This is a time of crisis, the bourgeoisie are the ruling class, they can no longer rule in the "old way", and they have decided to "change their method of rule". They have decided to set Trump up as a dictator.

In a very short time, the situation has changed dramatically. It is doubtful that there will be a federal election in November, or if there is such an election, it will likely be pointless. The bourgeoisie have almost certainly decided that Trump will continue as "president", but with unlimited powers. He is one of their own, a fellow billionaire, and they can count on him to protect them.

No doubt other states will form other coalitions, or possibly join the coalitions which already exist. For their own safety, they are being forced into this. There is safety in numbers. It is very likely that Trump will send federal troops into states which he considers to be "mutinous", with the intention of hanging the governors of those states, as well as anyone else who dares defy him. It will no doubt come as a comfort to know that member states are about to come to their aid. This is another way of saying that *America is on the brink of another civil war!* Now it is up to conscious people, Marxists, to transform this approaching civil war into a revolutionary war, a class war, a war for scientific socialism, a war for the Dictatorship of the Proletariat.

Trump has already introduced a "three phase plan" to open up the country, because as he put it, "there has to be a balance… there's also death involved in keeping it closed". He neglected to point out just what death was "involved in keeping it closed". Trump is merely focused in opening up the country, returning to "business as usual". He refuses to face the fact that those "good old days" are gone, never to return.

Perhaps the idea of American troops invading states will be sufficient to motivate conscious people, those who are aware of the revolutionary theories of Marx and Lenin, to become active. A Communist Party is desperately needed. That is the one and only Party which can provide the proletariat with the leadership they need. All other parties will merely steer the revolution onto the bourgeois path. Recall the words of Lenin: *"Without a revolutionary theory, there can be no revolutionary motion"*. (my italics)

Trump has already been busy, hurling insults at various governors who have the gall to stand up to him. He appears to have a particular hatred for the governors of New York and Washington state. He is calling for citizens of those states, among others, to defy the bans on social distancing and to not stay at home. The governors are in turn confused and frustrated, as Trump consistently contradicts himself, first saying one thing one day and the exact opposite the next. Crazy or not, he is clearly not stable.

Any day now Trump could send troops into states which he perceives to be "mutinous". It is not clear that those troops would obey his orders. It is clear that such an act would likely cause the start of a civil war. Perhaps the thought of American troops invading American states will inspire American intellectuals, working class as well as middle class, to do that which needs to be done.

Form a Communist Party.

35

MOSASAURS, PLESIOSAURS, ICHTHYOSAURS ET. AL.

For many years, I have been searching for various orders of prehistoric reptiles. Within each order, there are no doubt numerous species. The flying reptiles are referred to as pterosaurs, and are divided into those with long tails, called rhamphorinchus, and those with short tails, called pterodactyl. The long tailed species are far more numerous. All are predators, as well as nocturnal, which is to say that they avoid the light, spending all the day light hours in caves. They hunt in darkness, and as is characteristic of all predators, they have a keen sense of smell. As is also characteristic of predators, they are far more likely to attack when they smell blood. For that reason, they frequently prey upon females of child bearing age. They also prey upon children, as youngsters are easier to pick up and carry away.

These flying reptiles *did not go extinct* sixty five million years ago. They are very much alive and preying upon us, to this day. That is a fact, just as it is a fact that there are four orders of swimming reptiles which are also very much alive. They also prey upon us. These include the mosasaurs, ichthyosaurs, long necked plesiosaurs and short necked plesiosaurs. Within each order there are numerous species. Now it is just a matter of proving they exist.

I am sure that the various species of swimming reptiles have adapted to life in fresh water as well as salt water. I am also sure that the freshwater reptiles are nocturnal, and I strongly suspect that the same is true of the salt water reptiles. At the same time, I am no longer sure that all of the swimming reptiles lay eggs. The scientists suspect that at least some of them give birth to live young.

In particular, the animal in Okanagan Lake, also known as ogopogo, matches the description of the ichthyosaur. It is the scientific opinion that this reptile went extinct eighty million years ago. It is my opinion that they are completely mistaken.

I was also of the opinion that almost all reptiles lay eggs. The exceptional ones carry eggs inside their bodies until they hatch, then give birth to live young. Of course most reptiles are not exceptional, so it logically follows that the easiest way to prove the existence of these swimming reptiles is to locate the eggs they lay. As they lay eggs in sand, the easiest way to locate this nesting site is to keep an eye out for birds of prey, which gather immediately before the eggs hatch. Locate the flocks of birds of prey and locate the nesting sites. These birds of prey are referred to as raptors. All quite simple, or so I thought.

My investigation into the Okanagan Lake monster, opopogo, has left me puzzled, at least at first. Numerous eye witness accounts agree on the size and shape of the animal, among other things. Videos support these accounts. Yet people who live around the lake, swear that the only sand on the beaches has been trucked into the sites. There is no naturally occurring sand on those beaches, merely gravel. As that is the case, there is no way the ichthyosaurs can lay their eggs in gravel. The one and only alternative is that it must give birth to live young.

That being the case, the animal must either be a mammal, or perhaps a reptile with characteristics of mammals, in that it gives birth to live young. It is extremely unlikely to be a mammal, as pound for pound, mammals require ten times as much nourishment as reptiles. As this is a very large animal, it is very unlikely that one lake could support a population of such mammals. I am still convinced that it is a reptile.

Further research has revealed that there are fossils of the ichthyosaur which suggest the animal gives birth to live young. Even more surprising, it is clear that the animal gives birth head first. In that case, it is necessary for the animal to come out of the water to give birth, as otherwise the youngster would drown, in the process of being born.

Now the problem is one of locating the beach where the animal gives birth. This may not be as difficult as it sounds, as in this case also, it is very likely that birds of prey will gather. Not that the raptors are likely to prey upon the youngster, but the act of giving birth is bound to give rise to other material, referred to as afterbirth, which is merely food for predators.

It is possible that this lake is exceptional in that there is no naturally occurring sand along the beaches, and that is the reason the ichthyosaur can survive here. Perhaps the other apex predators, mosasaurs and plesiosaurs, lay eggs and therefore require sandy beaches. If that is the case, then this animal has no competition, at least not in Okanagan Lake. That remains to be seen.

From the fossilized remains of mosasaurs and plesiosaurs, it is not clear how they reproduce. It is very likely that they lay eggs, as do most reptiles, but that has yet to be determined. Either way, it is still my opinion that the best way to locate these animals, in fresh water or salt water, is to look for their nesting sites. The gathering of birds of prey, raptors, is sure to take place. As far as these raptors are concerned, there is no difference between freshly hatched eggs and the "after birth" of an animal. Both are food.

From our viewpoint, that of humans, it is every bit as urgent to prove the existence of these swimming reptiles, as it is of proving the existence of the flying reptiles. All are predators, they prey upon us, and it is vital that the members of the public be notified. To be fore warned is to be fore armed.

For this reason, I am appealing to the members of the public to assist in locating these reptiles. The scientists either cannot or will not do this. Now it is up to us. Countless lives are at stake. Together, we can make a difference.

37

DEPRESSION: A CRISIS OF ABUNDANCE

As I write this, the official death toll, as a result of the corona virus, has reached 44,000. In one week, the death toll has doubled. The true death toll is far higher, as those who choose to die at home, surrounded by family, are not counted in the "official" toll. For this reason, there are fewer admissions to hospitals and the "curve is flattening", to use the stilted language of the government officials.

A more accurate picture is presented by the World Health Organization, WHO. An official from that agency stated quite clearly that the "worst is yet to come". As well, the Centre for Disease Control, CDC, expects a second wave of the virus this winter, which "could be worse", as it will likely strike at the same time as the flu epidemic.

As well, the country is entering a deep Depression, one which is expected to be even more intense than the Great Depression of the previous century. The government has responded to these twin crises by spending *trillions of dollars*, which is thousands of billions, on that which it refers to as "economic stimulus packages". It is also calling for an end to the "stay at home" orders and to the "social distancing" policies, in an attempt to "jump start" the economy.

The press is mainly focused on the havoc caused by the corona virus, and the various plans to reopen the economy. There is even the occasional interview with economists, those who do their best Guy Smiley imitations. Such economists ignore the fact that the country is now head over heels in debt, facing bankruptcy. Millions of small businesses are ruined, and the rest are hanging on by their finger tips. Millions of workers are now unemployed, with a great many more about to join them. As soon as the government hand outs run out, the rest of the small businesses will face bankruptcy. The employees and the owners will soon join the many millions of unemployed. There is simply no way out of this Depression.

This is a true crisis in capitalism, technically referred to as an economic crisis compounded by a medical crisis. Such economic crises occur periodically, as the capitalists produce "too much". This gives rise to a surplus of goods. According to the "law of supply and demand", a great supply tends to reduce prices, while a great scarcity tends to raise prices. The capitalists love scarcity, as it tends to raise prices and consequently profits. By contrast, an over abundance tends to reduce prices and profits suffer.

I am writing this for the benefit of the working class people, proletarians, those who are just now becoming politically active. Those who were formerly members of the middle class, petty bourgeois, are already well aware of this, as they used any and all scarcities to their advantage.

Now we have a great abundance of most commodities while at the same time we have a severe shortage of certain other commodities. The contrast between the price of oil and the price of medical equipment is most striking. We now have so much oil it has been reduced to a *negative value!* The stock traders now report that a barrel of oil is now worth less than nothing! On the other hand, the price of medical equipment has increased ten fold!

The corona virus pandemic has forced governments around the world to encourage their citizens to stay at home and to practice "social distancing". As a result of this, people are using less gasoline. This contributes to the glut of oil on the market. At the same time, the "first responders", as well as medical personnel, require personal protective equipment, or PPE, as the virus is so contagious. So now the capitalists are making a great fortune from the sale of medical equipment.

The point must be driven home to working people that this economic Depression was not caused by the virus. The virus is a crisis in itself, a medical crisis, which is causing the Depression to be more intense. The problem is not that society has too little. The problem is that we now have *too much!* We have a vast surplus, and this, from the standpoint of the capitalists, is a disaster.

It may be objected that under monopoly capitalism, the capitalists can come together and agree to limit the supply, thereby ensuring a continuous shortage. They certainly make every attempt to do just that. The organization known as OPEC, Organization of Petroleum Exporting Countries, was set up with that in mind. The trouble being that the capitalists of all countries have one characteristic in common. All are completely devoid of principle.

Each and every capitalist has the moral fibre of a mobster. They do not hesitate to "cut the throat" of the other, as that is the term they use. All are determined to "make a buck", so that their word is meaningless. They can and do "turn on a dime" on each other.

That is one side of the coin, or as Marxists are fond of putting it, one aspect of the contradiction. The other side is the fact that many millions of working people, those who have formerly been apathetic, are now "awake", politically active, more consciously aware and determined to enact change. Now is the time to raise that level of awareness, to make them aware of themselves as a class, with their own class interests, which is diametrically opposed to the interests of the capitalists, the bourgeoisie.

That is the point where Marxists come into the picture. It is up to Marxists to raise the level of awareness of the proletariat. The best way to do this is through the use of specific examples, and not mere "preaching", the use of revolutionary phrases. That may sound rather harsh, and perhaps it is. The fact remains that working people get tired of listening to the same old expressions, which may be revolutionary but remain a bore. The contrast between the price of oil and the price of medical equipment is anything but a bore.

That contrast should get the attention of working people. Then the fact can be presented that under capitalism, a surplus is a curse, while under socialism, a surplus can only be a bonus. The idea is to go from the particular to the general. The particular should be of interest to people, and rest assured, the prices of gasoline and medical equipment is of interest to almost everyone.

Once a Marxist has the attention of an individual, or a group of people, their attention can be drawn to the general. Point out the fact that the ruling class, the monopoly capitalists, the bourgeoisie, are not about to give up their wealth and power without a fight. That is the reason it is necessary to overthrow them through revolution. After that, it is also necessary to crush them under the Dictatorship of the Proletariat.

As for those who may object that the working people are not capable of understanding this, may I suggest that you do not know too much about working people. The only reason the members of the working class are not discussing the Dictatorship of the Proletariat is because they are as yet not aware of this! It is up to Marxists to bring this awareness to the working class. Bear in mind that as Lenin pointed out, *"without a revolutionary theory, there can be no revolutionary motion"!*

Currently the middle class, the petty bourgeois, is in the process of being wiped out. Many of those people are aware of the revolutionary theories of Marx and Lenin. Now is the time to "spread the word", to let your fellow proletariats know of those theories. Face the fact that you are no longer middle class. Those days are "gone with the wind", never to return.

Prepare for the Dictatorship of the Proletariat.

37

AN APPEAL TO WORKING PEOPLE

The confirmed deaths due to the corona virus has now surpassed the number of Americans killed in the Viet Nam war. The confirmed cases of the virus, in America alone, is now over one million. The chief adviser to the president, his own son in law, is now referring to the response by the federal government as a "great victory". That is one way to put it, although I can think of others. The term "national disgrace" comes to mind. The total number of deaths due to the virus is far higher than the "confirmed cases", as so many people prefer to die at home, surrounded by family, rather than alone in a hospital.

The press is now reporting that within the last six weeks, thirty million working people have applied for unemployment insurance benefits. That number is expected to rise dramatically as ever more businesses go broke. For the moment, a great many small businesses are able to meet their payroll due to government grants, referred to as Economic Stimulus Packages. Another such package has just been approved by the federal government, to the tune of half a trillion dollars. The last such package, of a few hundred billion, lasted only a few weeks, so this one will not last long either. When that money runs out, many more "small businesses" will in turn go broke, resulting in more unemployment.

It should be noted that a "small business" is defined as a business employing less than five hundred people. There are a great many such businesses which are merely subsidiaries of huge corporations. The money given to them is nothing less than corporate welfare. All of this comes at tax payer expense, of course.

The governors of various states are calling for money to support the hospitals and medical support agencies. The federal government is aware of the severe financial hardship caused by the virus and the Depression. Their response, as clearly stated by the minority leader of the Senate, is that "it is better for the states to go bankrupt, rather than be funded by the federal government". Even the federal leaders are aware that the country is facing bankruptcy, and as that is the case, are prepared to allow the individual states to go broke instead. It is to the credit of the minority leader that he has blurted out the fact, which the federal government is trying to keep secret, that they plan to allow the states to go broke. Every so often the loyal servants of the bourgeoisie speak the truth.

Trump is also calling for people to use disinfectant to combat the corona virus. It is not clear if he is suggesting that people drink this poison or to "mainline it", to use a needle to shoot it into their veins. Either approach is sure to be most unpleasant, possibly fatal. Even for Trump, it was a stupid thing to say. Then again, possibly it was merely a typical Trump statement. Just as typical of Trump is the fact that he now denies saying precisely the thing he said. Perhaps that is his idea of damage control.

The press is now pointing out that it is routine for Trump to lie. As soon as the press points out one lie, the members of his staff -belly crawling boot lickers, one and all- come out with a separate set of lies, as a separate means of damage control. Then Trump denies his original lie with an altogether new set of lies, in the process also contradicting the lies of his boot lickers. This may sound like political satire, but is the sad truth.

At least one of the states is heeding the call of Trump to open up for business. Such businesses as beauty shops, tattoo parlours and nail solons are now open, as part of a "phased reopening" of the state. So on the one hand, citizens are being advised to stay at home, except those who are working in "essential services". All are being advised to exercise "social distancing". Those who are not working in essential services are being advised to leave their homes only for purposes of shopping for groceries or emergency medical appointments. On the other hand, they are being encouraged to go for a hair cut, get a tattoo and manicure. Just how they are expected to get their hair cut, a tattoo and manicure while staying home and exercising social distancing, is not clear.

Citizens of various states are heeding the call of Trump to protest "social distancing". It is the federal government, led by Trump, which is calling for social distancing, yet Trump is encouraging people to protest and defy this same order. There is an expression, to the effect of "be careful what you pray for, you may just get it". Trump would do well to take this to heart, as he may get what he wants. In spades, no less. These same protesters will likely turn against him, and capitalism in general, and start calling for revolution and a socialist republic. From there, it is a small step to calling for the Dictatorship of the Proletariat.

There are also reports of demonstrations in the state of Michigan, at the government building within the state capital. People there are protesting the "stay at home" orders. It is also reported that some of these protesters are also carrying firearms. If true, this is a huge escalation of the class conflict. This is especially significant as the state of Michigan is part of the industrial heartland of the country. We can expect the industrial proletariat to play a key role in the forthcoming revolution.

This is to drive home the point that the situation is revolutionary. We have a medical crisis caused by the virus, and a crisis of over production, which has given rise to a Depression. We have a great abundance, more than enough for everyone. Under capitalism, this is a terrible curse. It is only under socialism that a surplus is a great blessing.

People are protesting because they want jobs. Working people are proud, too proud to stay at home and receive hand outs. That is a fact, just as it is a fact that we currently live under capitalism. The capitalists are in charge, the billionaires, the bourgeoisie. They do not care what workers want. They care only about their profits.

As the title of this article suggests, I am writing this with working people in mind. I most sincerely hope to God that there are a great many such people who are reading this. Aside from the virus, we are entering a Depression, one which is anticipated to be more severe than the Great Depression of the twentieth century.

Our parents and grandparents suffered through that Depression for ten years. To give an idea of the desperation faced at that time, I can give the example of my father, who dug ditches for twenty five cents an hour. Perhaps the billionaires of today think that our generation will also tolerate such massive unemployment, hunger and disease. If that is the case, they are sadly mistaken.

The one and only way out of this Depression is through *scientific socialism*. This stands in stark contrast to utopian socialism. The difference is that scientific socialism is based upon the scientific theories of Marx and Lenin. Those theories have been proven to be correct. Experience has shown that revolutions which follow the advice of Marx and Lenin are successful, while revolutions which do not follow their advice always fail.

The fact is that the working class, technically referred to as the proletariat, *must overthrow the capitalist class and crush them under the Dictatorship of the Proletariat!*

Notice that I have deliberately used capital letters to stress the importance of that Dictatorship. That is a strong term, no ifs, ands or buts. It is also a fundamental tenet of Marxism that there is no other way to establish socialism. Bitter experience has proven that, beyond any shadow of a doubt. Any and all revolutions which have taken place, without crushing the bourgeoisie under the iron rule of the proletariat, *have failed!*

The capitalists, the billionaires, the bourgeoisie, are well aware of this. In fact, the Dictatorship of the Proletariat is their worst night mare. The middle class people, the small business owners, the petty bourgeois, are also aware of this. Most of them are now ruined, or about to be ruined, and are joining the ranks of the working class. It is up to middle class intellectuals to bring this awareness to the working class. By and large, this is not happening, so that calls for an alternative. There is more than one way to skin a cat.

Most working people are literate and have personal computers. Those of us who grew up with rotary telephones may not be terribly proficient with those computers, but our grandchildren are available to help us out. Just take my advice and do not try to explain the finer points of rotary phones. There are certain things the younger generation simply cannot understand. Perhaps that is just as well. Besides, being referred to as a dinosaur can become rather tiresome.

With that in mind, may I suggest to fellow working people that a careful reading of the Essential Works of Lenin is a fine place to start. Imperialism, the Highest Stage of Capitalism, is quite easy to understand, and gives a fine idea of the problem we are facing, that of monopoly capitalism. Then State and Revolution explains the importance of smashing the existing state machine, that which has been set up by the capitalists, the bourgeoisie, in order to crush the working class, the proletariat. Such a state apparatus must be replaced by an entirely different set up, a proletarian apparatus, in order to smash the "desperate and determined" resistance of the bourgeoisie. As well, the book What Is To Be Done?, explains the resistance we can expect to encounter, among those who claim to be socialists or Marxists or Communists, but are opposed to the Dictatorship of the Proletariat. At the moment, that is almost all "socialist" parties.

That should give working people a fine understanding of the basic principles of Marxism. It is certainly a place to start. Then such workers can advise their friends and coworkers. As well, the internet is available, with various "social networking" sites, assuming that is the correct term. In this way, the level of awareness among the working class can be raised. No doubt the most advanced workers will be raised to the level of true Marxists. There is no time to waste, as the revolution could break out any day now.

Having said that, there is no way to predict the exact day of the revolution. Our task now is to prepare for the revolution and the subsequent Dictatorship of the Proletariat. Working people, proletarians, *must* learn the skills in leadership now, which they will need after the revolution. For that reason I encourage working people to become active in working class organizations of all sorts, from trade unions to sewing circles. As well, feel free to join the two mainstream political parties, as card carrying members, and run for any and all political office, on behalf of both parties.

The fact is that at the time of the revolution, *leaders will emerge!* Many of these leaders will be servants of the bourgeoisie, boot lickers one and all. They will try to divert the revolution onto some harmless path of social reform, away from the Dictatorship of the Proletariat. Many of them will do this in the name of Marx and Lenin, no less. They must be opposed. That is where true leaders of the working class come into the picture, proletarian leaders. This is not to imply that such leaders must be working class. Bear in mind that both Marx and Lenin were middle class, members of the intelligentsia. To be prejudiced against middle class intellectuals is to be prejudiced against Marx and Lenin! The important thing is not the class background, but the *class they serve!*.

This is to say that a true Marxist political party, a Communist Party, must be formed. Only such a party can provide the working class, the proletariat, with the leadership, the direction, it so desperately needs. Usually it is the middle class intellectuals who take part in the creation of such a party. As yet, that is not happening. Or if it is, it is a well kept secret, which only defeats the purpose. We need a Communist Party, one which openly calls for the Dictatorship of the Proletariat. As that is the case, and as middle class intellectuals are not performing their duty, it is up to working class intellectuals to rise to the occasion.

Proletarian intellectuals are few in number, but they do exist. The important thing is quality, not quantity. They have also been schooled in the class struggle. If nothing else, bitter experience has taught them about the conflict between the classes. Not a great deal of persuasion is required to convince them that the capitalists must be crushed under the Dictatorship of the Proletariat. Now it is a little matter of raising their level of consciousness to that of Marxists. Then they can take part in the formation of a proper Communist Party.

Now is not the time for false modesty. Such advanced workers know who they are. To such proletarians I can only say, spare all of us the "aw, shucks, I'm just a simple country boy" routine. Now is not the time for a song and dance. Now is the time for working class leaders to come forward and give direction. Your own people, your working class, is counting upon you.

As for those who think that we can have a political party which will represent all citizens, regardless of class, you are mistaken. We live in a class society, so any political party stands for the proletariat or it stands for the bourgeoisie. There is no alternative, no middle ground. At present, we live under the dictatorship of the bourgeoisie. After the revolution, the only way to establish socialism is through the Dictatorship of the Proletariat.

We will know that we are being successful in getting our message to working people when various Marxist slogans are commonplace:

Scientific Socialism!
Dictatorship of the Proletariat!
Workers of the World, Unite!
Victory or Death!

38

TOWARDS A WORLD SOCIALIST REPUBLIC

The number of "confirmed" deaths, due to the corona virus, is now over 70,000. There are a great many unconfirmed deaths, due to the corona virus, but the government prefers not to recognize them. Most of the states are now beginning a "process of phased reopening", as they explained it. At the same time, the number of daily cases of confirmed deaths, due to the virus, has reached an all time high. The medical professionals expect the daily death rate to possibly double as states "reopen", people mingle, and the virus has a better chance to spread.

As the virus runs its deadly course, the Second Great Depression also takes root. Within the last several weeks, thirty million workers have filed for benefits. That number is expected to rise dramatically as ever more small businesses file for bankruptcy. As well, various states are also close to that point, and are already in the process of laying off workers. For that matter, the federal government is in danger of going broke, although the officials are reluctant to admit this.

The working people are rapidly approaching the point of desperation. So many people are living paycheck to paycheck, and those paychecks are running out. As a result, people are being faced with the choice of paying rent or putting food on the table. The government officials have graciously decided to bless the fortunate few with paltry handouts, which merely delays the day when so many people will lose their homes.

Working people are rising up, in violation of any "stay at home" orders, as well as any "social distancing" orders. In the state capital of Michigan, armed protesters made this abundantly clear. As well, in the state capital of California, protesters also gathered, but without any firearms. As these citizens were not such a threat, the government officials became quite brave and arrested a great many of them.

People are protesting more than just "social distancing". They are convinced that the government is doing next to nothing to prevent the spread of the virus, and even less in trying to find a cure for the sickness. As well, workers want jobs. There is an increasing awareness, or at least a growing suspicion, that nothing is about to change. If the government has its way, that is precisely the way it will remain.

Under these conditions, it is only natural that thoughts of socialism should enter the minds of people. It is also only natural that the capitalists, the billionaires, technically referred to as the bourgeoisie, should respond that socialism, or Communism, has been tried, and has been proven to be a disaster. They then give the examples of Russia and China.

In fact, I have personally spoken to numerous people from Eastern Europe, those who are clearly not "Communists", but have lived in "Communist countries". These people, workers one and all, say that "Communism is not what Lenin thought it would be". In this, they are absolutely correct.

This calls for a little explanation. It is true that the Russian Revolution of October, 1917, gave birth to a socialist republic, in that the bourgeoisie were crushed under the working class, the Dictatorship of the Proletariat. A similar thing happened in China, after the Chinese Revolution of 1948. Since that time, in each country, the capitalists, the bourgeoisie, have managed to return to power. In Russia, or the USSR, as it was then called, this happened after the death of Stalin. In China, the capitalists returned to power after the death of Mao.

This does not mean that scientific socialism, the revolutionary theories of Marx and Lenin, are not valid. It does mean that *after* the revolution, *after* the billionaires are separated from their wealth and power, *after* they are deprived of their life of luxury, after they are no longer being waited upon hand and foot, *then* their rage, their fury, their hatred, will rise to heights which cannot be imagined, at least not by mere mortals. *After* these people are "reduced" to the state of "paupers", a state of life which they never imagined, a state in which they are forced to "work for their daily bread", "degraded" to the lot of common toilers, *then* they will make every effort, they will resort to any length, any subterfuge, they will spare no lies, in an attempt to return to power.

That is precisely the thing which happened in Russia and China. The capitalists of those countries went to the extreme length of pretending to be Communists, infiltrated the Communist Parties of each country, and managed to restore capitalism.

Strangely enough, this is not as surprising as it may sound. It was Lenin who pointed out that it is far less difficult to start a revolution in a "petty bourgeois" country, but far more difficult to carry it through in successive stages. By contrast, it is far more difficult to start a revolution in "developed" countries, but far easier to carry it through in successive stages.

A developed country is far more cultured, so that the bourgeois influence is far more wide spread. By contrast, most people in a petty bourgeois country, as was Russia in 1917, were illiterate peasants. Those peasants were less exposed to the bourgeois influence.

Lenin explained that in 1917 Russia, the "overwhelming majority" of the population was "petty bourgeois". I found this rather surprising as it was my idea that small business owners are middle class or petty bourgeois. That is true, but Lenin pointed out that the vast majority of peasants are also "small proprietors" and can be "nothing else…They have not been schooled; their economic and political conditions do not bring them together, but rather tend to separate, alienating them from each other, and transforming them into millions of lone wolf small proprietors". This is to say that all peasants, even the most poverty stricken, are small time capitalists!

At the time of the October revolution in Russia, all peasants were united in their hatred of the landlords. As the landlords were the allies of the nobility, as well as the capitalists, the bourgeoisie, the revolution was against all of these classes. This made the peasants the natural allies of the working class, the proletariat. Immediately after the revolution, the landlords were stripped of their property and the land belonged to the tiller. This is referred to as the land socialization law, so that the land the peasant was tilling belonged to him. Further, much of the equipment, such as draft animals and tractors, was distributed to the poor peasants.

This is certainly not socialism, but under the circumstances, a step forward. It was simply not reasonable to expect the peasants to embrace socialized, collective farming. They only gradually became aware of this, so that it took time and patience. In the mean time, the capitalists did their best to "stir the pot", to "cause trouble", to spread discontent.

It is partly for this reason that the capitalists were able to restore capitalism in Russia, after the death of Stalin, and to restore capitalism in China, after the death of Mao. This is no reason for despair. This does not mean that we are destined to endure capitalism until the end of time. This does mean that we have got to learn from the mistakes of previous revolutions.

The current situation is far different, at least in North America. The capitalists have succeeded in simplifying the class conflict. The family farmers, the American equivalent of the European peasant, have been all but wiped out, although a few are still in existence. The vast majority of small businesses, the petty bourgeois, are either broke or going broke. That leaves the working class, the proletariat, and the capitalists, the bourgeoisie. That narrows it right down. It also means that the revolution is far more difficult to start, but once started, will not face the resistance from the petty bourgeois, as the class of people we refer to as the petty bourgeois, has been all but wiped out.

Now comes the not so little matter of starting the revolution, which is very difficult in a developed country, although perhaps not as difficult as in previous years. As Lenin stated it, "It is much more difficult to start a revolution in West European countries because there the revolutionary proletariat is opposed by the higher thinking that comes with culture, and the working class is in a state of cultural slavery". He also explained that "the culture of the advanced countries has been, and still is, the result of their being able to live at the expense of a thousand million people." As a result of the export of capital, "the capitalists of these countries obtain a great deal more in this way than they could obtain as profits by plundering the workers in their own countries...out of this tidy sum, at least five hundred millions can be spent as a sop to the labour leaders and the labour aristocracy, on all sorts of bribes. The whole thing boils down to *nothing but bribery*. ...In America, Britain and France we see a far greater persistence of the opportunist leaders, of the upper crust of the working class, the labour aristocracy; they offer stronger resistance to the Communist movement... the purging of the workers parties, the revolutionary parties of the proletariat all over the world, of bourgeois influences, of the opportunists in their ranks, is very far from complete... Opportunism is our principle enemy. Opportunism in the upper ranks of the working class movement is *bourgeois socialism, not proletarian socialism*. It has been shown in practice that *working class activists who follow the opportunist trend are better defenders of the bourgeoisie than the bourgeoisie themselves*. Without their leadership of the workers, *the bourgeoisie could not remain in power*...This is where our principle enemy is, an enemy we must overcome." (my italics)

I should add, for the benefit of those who are just now becoming politically active, that opportunism merely means unprincipled or dishonest. As Lenin has pointed out, there is no shortage of that scum in the working class. The capitalists are quite adept at identifying such people, those whom are generally referred to as "trouble makers". They are then offered a bribe of one sort or another. Those who accept are "off to the races", in the "pocket of the capitalists", referred to as "labour lieutenants of the capitalist class". They soon become devoted servants of the bourgeoisie, earning every dime of their pay.

Then along comes a crisis and there is weeping and wailing in the land of the class traitors. Our present crisis comes as twins, in the form of a virus and a Depression. The profits of the capitalists have been reduced dramatically and they have responded by cutting expenses. The bribes are an expense, and they have been suspended, or at least dramatically reduced. Hence the crying of the class traitors, true crocodile tears.

As I have mentioned in previous articles, now is the time for working class people to become active. Prepare for the Dictatorship of the Proletariat. Assume leadership positions in working class organizations, especially trade unions, but also sports clubs and any other organization. As well, become card carrying members of the two mainstream political parties. Run for any and all political office, on behalf of both parties. Study the Essential Works of Lenin, and prepare to form a true Communist Party, one which calls for the Dictatorship of the Proletariat.

Without such a party, it is doubtful that the revolution can succeed. Membership in the Communist Party must be exclusive, as only such a Party can give the required leadership. By contrast, we want to have as many working people behind us as possible, from all walks of life, in as many organizations as possible, everything from trade unions to mainstream political parties.

All of this is a tall order, but we have to start some where. Feel free to draw inspiration from the words of Lenin: "World imperialism shall fall when the revolutionary onslaught of the exploited and oppressed workers in each country, overcoming resistance from petty bourgeois elements and the influence of the small upper crust of labour aristocrats, merges with the revolutionary onslaught of hundreds of millions of people who have hitherto stood beyond the pale of history, and have been regarded merely as the object of history."

The current situation is such that the virus has spread around the world, and is causing widespread devastation. As well, the Depression is adding to the suffering of countless people. It is clear that many of the countries which are being hit very hard are the same countries which are the most developed. It is a fact that a successful socialist revolution in all of those countries, or at least many of them, will make a huge difference. It will be a big step towards a World Socialist Republic.

Assuming that the revolution is successful in all, or at least several advanced countries, it is a mistake to assume that the capitalist stage of economic development is inevitable for under developed countries. Lenin was asked such a question, and he replied: "If the victorious revolutionary proletariat conducts systematic propaganda among them, and the Soviet governments come to their aid with all the means at their disposal -in that event it will be mistaken to assume that the backward peoples must inevitably go through the capitalist stage of development....with the aid of the proletariat of the advanced countries, backward countries can go over to the Soviet system and, through certain stages of development, to Communism, without having to pass through the capitalist stage."

It is clear that the revolutionary motion is raging in several countries of the world. In North America, it is being led by women, if only because so many working class leaders are men, and many of them have been bribed by the bourgeoisie. As those bribes are drying up, it may well be not so difficult to expose them and remove them from positions of authority. Not that it will be easy, as people who are in such positions generally get the idea that it is their God given right to rule.

On the other hand, as Lenin pointed out, "The experience of all liberation movements has shown that the success of a revolution depends on how much the women take part it it." In North America, the women are leading the revolution. Well done, ladies! Now is no time to be shy. Place no restrictions on yourself. Exercise the talents you have, whether it is in the field of entertainment, organization, music or writing, to name a few. As well, study the essential works of Lenin. There is no time like the present to learn Marxist revolutionary theory. You have distinguished yourselves in the recent past, so build upon that which you have started. Like it or not, countless people are counting on you. How is that for pressure?

Without doubt, the revolutionary motion is also taking place in other parts of the world. At the moment, the press is focused mainly on the corona virus, so it is difficult to obtain any particular facts on the subject.

We just have to do out part, in preparation for the revolution and the subsequent Dictatorship of the Proletariat. Perhaps that will serve as an inspiration for other revolutionaries in other parts of the world. Or perhaps they are doing their part too, and it is just not being reported.

It may help to give some thought to Rosa Luxemburg, one of the martyrs to the cause. She devoted her life to the cause of scientific socialism, to the emancipation of the working class, to the emancipation of women. As she put it, "the working class has nothing to lose but their chains". With her memory in mind, may I suggest another slogan:

Victory or Death!

39

THREE TRENDS IN THE REVOLUTIONARY MOVEMENT

The contradictions in the world of capitalism are becoming ever more intense. Now even the journalists are daring to mention that capitalism is in a state of crisis. They are further reporting that unemployment is at a level which has not been seen since the days of the Great Depression. There is currently a great abundance, a vast surplus of almost all commodities. Under socialism this is a great blessing, but as we live under capitalism, it is considered to be a terrible curse, in that prices have been driven down. The business reporters are suggesting that profits have been "negatively impacted", which is to say that the capitalists are losing money.

As well, the corona virus is causing death and devastation on a scale not seen since the days of the flu epidemic of a century ago. Of the confirmed number of dead due to the virus, roughly a quarter of them are confined to one country, which is America. In fact the official death toll in that country is approaching 100,000. As well, tens of millions of people in the same country are currently unemployed. The ruling class, the billionaires, the bourgeoisie, are at their wits end, not sure of which way to jump.

The government first responded to the twin crises by shutting down the country, aside from essential services, and initiating various "economic stimulus packages", in an attempt to get the country "back on its feet". The latest such package, approved by the House of Representatives, amounts to *3 trillion dollars*. If approved, this will send the national debt to heights never before imagined, possibly 30 trillion dollars. Of course, that is just the debt the government chooses to acknowledge. They manage to keep the national debt at artificially low levels, by simply denying the existence of money they owe.

Now the government has decided to initiate "limited reopening", in an attempt to further "stimulate the economy". This has also resulted in further "stimulating the virus", in that hospitals are reporting an increase in the number of patients who are suffering from the virus. We can count on the bourgeoisie to deal with a situation which is desperate and transform it into an absolute disaster.

This is another way of saying that the situation is truly revolutionary, as the ruling class, the bourgeoisie, can no longer rule in the old way. As well, the class which is being ruled, the proletariat, is no longer content to be ruled in any manner. They are rising up, demanding change, holding their leaders accountable. At least, they are making a supreme effort.

In response to these twin crises in capitalism, President Trump has managed to scale the twin peaks of stupidity and incompetence. His latest brainstorm is to declare religious services as "essential services", and to order the buildings of all such religions, whether churches, mosques or synagogues, to be opened. He is also threatening to override any governor who dares to disobey that order.

The journalists are reporting that Trump does not have that authority, as no where does the Constitution grant him that power. That is certainly true, yet those same journalists are overlooking the fact that Trump declared that he has "total power". He was not joking. He was also not joking when he said that any governor who dared challenge his authority was committing a "mutiny". He "welcomes mutiny", and promises to be harsh with the mutineers. The various governors of the states, as well as any one else who dares to cross Trump, would do well to bear in mind that he has just threatened such people with death by hanging, as that is the penalty for mutiny.

Incredibly enough, it is just possible that the spark which sets off the American revolution, or at least the break up of the country, could well be the presidential directive to reopen the religious buildings!

Cracks are now appearing in the American empire. A number of states on each coast have come together in alliances, to form the nucleus of two republics. These are the two major population centres. As well, several states in the midwest, the industrial heart land of the country, have also come together, to form the nucleus of a third republic.

As mentioned in a previous article, the breaking up of the American empire and socialist revolution is on the horizon. Trump is doing his best to hasten the collapse of capitalism, at least in America. Now it is up to conscious people, Marxist intellectuals, to form a proper Communist Party. Working people need proper leaders, as they are not capable of setting up a scientific socialist society by themselves, a truly Marxist Dictatorship of the Proletariat. Their conditions of life do not lead to this awareness. This class consciousness can only be brought to them from conscious people, those who are aware of the revolutionary theories of Marx and Lenin.

In years gone by, that meant only middle class intellectuals were aware of those theories, and it was up to them to bring that awareness to the proletariat, to form a proper Communist Party. But now the situation has changed, in that most working people in America are literate and have access to the internet. As that is the case, I am encouraging all working people who are deeply discontent with the current situation to take action. By that I mean that all advanced workers, proletarians, must study the essential works of Lenin, raise their level of awareness and also take part in the creation of the Communist Party. Of course middle class intellectuals are also welcome to take part in creating the Party.

As members of that Party, they can expect to be faced with three trends in the revolutionary movement, according to Lenin. It is absolutely essential to recognize the existence of these trends and to fight consistently for the trend that is truly revolutionary.

The first trend is that of the social chauvinists, those who are socialists in words and chauvinists in deed. They may claim to be Marxist or Marxist -Leninist or Communists, while at the same time defending the bourgeoisie. They may or may not be members of a political party, while at the same time demanding nothing but paltry reforms. They absolutely do not demand anything that is not acceptable to the bourgeoisie. They are careful to not make any reference to revolution or to the Dictatorship of the Proletariat. They are MINO, Marxists In Name Only.

Historically, these people have generally not been members of the working class, the proletariat, but middle class intellectuals. That was before the virus and the Second Great Depression. Now the situation has changed quite dramatically. A great many middle class people have recently been ruined, forced into the ranks of the working class, and most of the remainder are soon to follow. That includes many of the social chauvinists, now being reduced to the level of proletarians. Now these former members of the middle class are joining their "comrades in arms", the upper stratum of the working class, those who have been bribed by the bourgeoisie. Together they do a fine job of defending the bourgeoisie, making every effort to divert the revolutionary motion onto some harmless path of social reform. As that is the case, these people, the social chauvinists, are the enemy.

As anyone with any considerable experience in the revolutionary movement can testify, there is no shortage of such people. They tend to be middle class, or at least of a middle class background, petty bourgeois. As the middle class is currently being wiped out in America, we can expect a great up surge of such people into the ranks of the proletariat, and into the class struggle. They may refer to themselves as Leftists, although most prefer the term Democratic Socialists or Independent Socialists. They tend to be well educated, aware of the revolutionary theories of Marx and Lenin, including the theory of the Dictatorship of the Proletariat.

Yet few of them are at all anxious to put those theories into practice. There is a big difference between being aware of the revolutionary theories and believing those same theories.

On occasion, individuals drift from one position to the other, from Centre to social chauvinist or the reverse, much as boats without anchors tend to drift around a lake. In fact, such people have no anchor, which is to say they take no guidance from the theories of Marx and Lenin.

This is not to say that the members of the centre are the enemy, because they are not. A great deal of patience is required in dealing with them, as they seem to be impervious to logic. No doubt their conditions of life, as members of the petty bourgeois, have led to this vacillating outlook on the class struggle, one day supporting the proletariat and the next day siding with the bourgeoisie. As the revolution gains strength, ever more of them will gravitate towards the proletariat.

This brings us to the third trend, and we will once again quote from Lenin, as it is so important. In reference to the third trend, he stated: "Its distinctive feature is its complete break with both social chauvinism and 'Centrism', and its gallant revolutionary struggle against *its own* imperialist government and *its own* imperialist bourgeoisie. Its principle is: 'Our chief enemy is at home'. It wages a ruthless struggle against honeyed social pacifist phrases (a social pacifist is a socialist in words and a bourgeois pacifist in deed; bourgeois pacifists dream of an everlasting peace *without* the overthrow of the yoke and domination of capital) and against all *subterfuges* employed to deny the possibility, or the appropriateness, or the timeliness of a proletarian revolutionary struggle and of a proletarian socialist revolution in connection with the present war".(all italics and punctuation by Lenin. It should be noted that this was written at the time of the great imperialist slaughter referred to as the First World War)

It is people who are members of this third trend who are destined to form a true Communist Party. It matters not if they have a petty bourgeois or a proletariat background. The important thing is that they are true Marxists, dedicated to scientific socialism, the revolution and the subsequent Dictatorship of the Proletariat. Their class background is of absolutely no consequence.

This is not to say that it is easy to be a Marxist, a member of the third trend, and to take part in forming a true Communist Party. It is not easy at all. That is a fact, just as it is a fact that certain things simply have to be done. May I suggest that those of you who are aware of the revolutionary theories of Marx and Lenin consider it your duty to take action, as it is your duty. As the old proverb states, "To whom much is given, of him much is required". To once again quote Lenin: "Such people are few; but it is on such people alone that the future of socialism depends; they *alone* are *the leaders of the people*, and not their corrupters…It is not a question of numbers, but of giving correct expression to the ideas and policies of the truly revolutionary proletariat". (italics by Lenin)

It is to be expected that the members of the public should be confused, if only because the social chauvinists make a supreme effort to spread confusion. It is for that reason I recommend the name of the party be Communist Party, Dictatorship of the Proletariat, or CP,DP. The social chauvinists are dead set opposed to the Dictatorship of the Proletariat, as it is the worst nightmare of their lords and masters, the bourgeoisie.

This should help to draw a clear distinction between the social chauvinists and the true Marxists.

May I suggest that Lenin wrote the previously quoted lines immediately before the German revolution of 1919, a revolution which spread across Western Europe. As is well known, that particular revolution was not successful, mainly because most of the leaders betrayed the working people and called for "defence of the fatherland", in support of their "own" bourgeoisie. Now it is up to American Marxists, true internationalists, to make sure that history does not repeat itself. There is only one way to do that:

Embrace the third trend. Form the Communist Party, Dictatorship of the Proletariat!

40

MERGER OF BLACK AND WORKING CLASS MOVEMENTS

The death of another unarmed Black man, at the hands of the police, has apparently triggered another American revolution. His murder was caught on video, by a bystander who recorded this on her cell phone. The video has gone "viral", and has been shown around the world. Countless people are outraged, not just in America but in numerous other countries. Protests have taken place all across America, in cities and small towns. Statues which have stood for years, in honour of such people as the Confederate General Robert E. Lee, are now being torn down. General Lee was a slave owner and staunch supporter of slavery. It was his firm belief that Black people were an inferior race, and he fought at the head of an army, in an effort to preserve the institution of slavery. Statues in honour of such people are an insult to all Black people, as well as to all minorities. For that matter, they are an insult to all those who fought for the Union in the Civil War. The sacrifice of those valiant soldiers should not be marred by honouring the memory the slave owners, the very people whom they destroyed.

The mass movement against violent police repression and racism has even spread overseas. In England, the statue of a man who lived several centuries ago was torn down and thrown into the river. The reason is that the statue honoured a man who was a slave trader. There too, the people are taking action, doing the "right thing", even if that right thing is not strictly within the absolute letter of the law. Some things just have to be done.

In America, the movement is very broad and deep. Even the journalists are now using the word revolution, if only in whispers, so to speak. It is clear that the word is cause for embarrassment. They are having a difficult time facing the fact that the current uprising, the protests, the marches, the calls for an end to police brutality and racism, is nothing less than a full scale revolution.

Never in the history of the country have so many distinguished figures, including former high ranking members of presidential administrations, as well as former high ranking military men, spoken out so clearly and passionately, against a sitting president.

One former four star general referred to the current protests as "the beginning of the end of the American experiment". This statement is perhaps not so much clear, as it is passionate.

It is characteristic of such people that they cannot bring themselves to use the word capitalism, much less socialism. The general used the expression "American experiment", as a reference to capitalism. Also, his expression "the beginning of the end" is a reference to the end of capitalism. Of course, it will soon be replaced by socialism, but that is a thought which the general finds too terrible for words.

A former Secretary of Defence referred to Trump as a "threat to the Constitution", someone who "tries to divide us". In this, he is absolutely correct.

The current Secretary of Defence has just openly disagreed with Trump on the question of using the American military against the protesters. The Defence Secretary considers it to be an "abuse of executive authority". Trump, by contrast, has no concept of abuse of executive authority. As far as he is concerned, he has absolute authority, and fully intends to use it, as he sees fit.

Even a high ranking member of the American Senate, a former candidate for the presidency and a member of the same political party as Trump, has marched with Black Lives Matter. He is perhaps the one and only such politician to go to that great length.

For the benefit of working people who are just now becoming politically active -welcome, my brothers and sisters, my comrades!- I will mention that there is a law referred to as the Posse Comitatus Act, which forbids the use of American military against American citizens. Trump responded to this by saying that the Insurrection Act of 1807 allows him to use the military within the country, in case of an "insurrection", as he sees fit. According to the same law, federal troops can be sent in to each state *only at the request of the governor* of that particular state. Trump has his own interpretation of the law. As far as he is concerned, if the governors are not doing their job, then he will do it for them!

Trump refers to himself as the "law and order president", yet his latest stunt made a mockery of law and order. In the interests of a "photo op", which is shorthand for photo opportunity, he had his Attorney General, the "top cop" in the country, clear an area, Lafayette Park, next to the White House, so that he could march to a nearby church and have his picture taken.

The park was occupied by peaceful protesters at that time, those who were exercising their democratic right to express their disapproval, as is guaranteed in the Constitution. The Attorney General of the country then gave the illegal order and the police responded by attacking those law abiding citizens with pepper spray, tear gas, shields and clubs. So much for law and order!

Trump then very proudly marched to the church and waved around a bible. He also posed with his closest aides. The journalists were quick to point out that all were White, although one of them was a female.

Trump is able to justify this by accusing all protesters of being "terrorists", members of an organization he refers to as Antifa. That is short for Anti Fascist, and very likely such an organization does not even exist. If it does exist, then it stands to reason that our parents and grandparents, those who fought the Nazis in World War 2, were terrorists! Such nonsense! It is also an insult to the millions of brave men and women who fought the fascist Nazis.

As mentioned in a previous article, cracks are beginning to appear in the American Empire. Several republics are starting to take shape. On the east coast and the west coast, the two population centres, states have come together. Also, in the midwest, the industrial heartland of the country, seven states have also formed an alliance. One of those states is Minnesota, home to Minneapolis, the city in which George Floyd was murdered. In other words, the epicentre of the revolution.

That is most significant, because the City Council of Minneapolis has just decided to take revolutionary action. In particular, they have decided to disband the Minneapolis City Police! They plan to replace it with a "new model of public safety". Now people across the country are calling for the "defunding" of various police agencies.

As for those who are confused concerning this "new model of public safety", there is a good reason for this. It has yet to take shape! It is a new creation of the revolution! The precise form it will assume remains to be seen.

The mayor of Minneapolis is dead set against this as he is in the service of the capitalists, but the City Council is reported to have a "veto proof majority".

It is to the credit of the journalists that they interviewed a young lady -clearly a leader- who stated that people were at first confused, suspecting that the police were not working the way they were supposed to work. But then they had second thoughts and came to the conclusion that the police are doing precisely that which they are supposed to be doing!

This is a huge step forward in the revolutionary working class movement. The members of the public are now aware, if only on an instinctive level, that the role of the police is *not to protect and serve* but to crush the working class! The police are nothing other than members of a state apparatus that is set up by the capitalists, the billionaires, the bourgeoisie, to crush the working class. It has nothing to do with "serve and protect"!

Now it is absolutely necessary to read the Essential Works of Lenin. May I suggest starting with State and Revolution, a book which was written immediately before the November 7 revolution of 1917. That was the revolution which brought the proletariat, the workers, to power in Russia. That book is as relevant now as it was then. Working people must be made aware that the capitalists, the billionaires, the bourgeoisie, are in charge. The capitalists make sure that the working people are kept under control. In fact, they have a fine apparatus set up to keep the working people suppressed. As Lenin put it, "A *standing army and police* are the chief instruments of state power". (my italics)

The point being that the more advanced members of the working class, the proletariat, are correct in thinking that the police are behaving precisely the way they are supposed to behave! They are the "chief instruments of state power"! It is the police and standing army, and in particular the National Guard, that is responsible for crushing the working class, the proletariat! It is the police and standing army that must be disbanded! Those are the "chief instruments of state power" which the capitalists use to crush the workers!

In Russia, 1917, it was only after the successful November revolution that the police and standing army were disbanded. Then the separate independent socialist republics took shape. At that time, it was first necessary to crush the capitalists under the newly created state apparatus, the Dictatorship of the Proletariat, and only then was it possible to disband the police and standing army.

By contrast, here in America, 2020, several independent republics are already taking shape. As well, the working people are more aware that the police are crushing them. Even before the revolution, they are taking the proper steps to disband the police departments. As the City Police are one of the "chief instruments of state power" of the capitalists, there can be no doubt that the capitalists will take a "dim view" of the attempt of the City Council to disband one of their most useful tools. The resistance the City Council is about to meet in trying to disband the City Police will prove to be most valuable training. This will serve them well after the revolution, as they assume positions of authority, under the Dictatorship of the Proletariat.

Further preparations must be made for the Dictatorship of the Proletariat. Workers, or at least the most advanced workers, must be encouraged to become members of any and all organizations, those which allow working class membership. This includes sports clubs, trade unions and political parties, especially the two mainstream parties, Democrats and Republicans. As card carrying members, party bosses, they can then run for any and all political offices. The purpose is to gain valuable experience in the class struggle, not to secure socialism through democratic elections. Regardless of what the social chauvinists say, socialism cannot be secured in that manner. On the other hand, such elections are a useful tool, to be used in the interests of raising the level of awareness of the working people.

There is also a desperate need for a true Marxist political party to lead the workers, the proletariat. Such a party can distinguish itself from the chauvinist parties by openly calling for the Dictatorship of the Proletariat.

As for those individuals who are referred to as "conscious people", which is to say people who are well aware of the revolutionary theories of Marx and Lenin, may I suggest that you perform your duty. To paraphrase the old expression, "to whom much has been given, from whom much is expected". You have the education and training. Use it. Feel free to form a true Marxist political party:

American Communist Party,
Dictatorship of the Proletariat

41

CREATE MORE AUTONOMOUS ZONES!

The working class movement has now merged with the Afro American movement, as well as with the struggle of all minorities, against violent police repression. Protesters are now marching all across the country, and for the most part, engaging in peaceful demonstrations. Criminal elements, vandals and looters, are of course taking advantage of the occasion to damage and thieve, but they are the exception.

The revolutionary motion is very broad and deep. In the city of Seattle, state of Washington, the protesters were so strong that the police in the East Precinct were forced to board up their detachment and abandon the building. The people then occupied several city blocks around the detachment. They are referring to this as the CHAZ, the Capital Hill Autonomous Zone. It is also being referred to as the Seattle Safe Zone, or the Seattle Commune. There is no visible police presence within the Zone.

This Zone or Commune is a *fundamental* political force, one which has grown out of the revolution. It is nothing less than a *workers government*, one which expresses the interest of the working class, the proletariat. As yet it is weak, very weak, but that in no way changes the fact that it is the embryo of a workers' government. For that reason, it requires our full support.

Protesters have hung a sign on the East Precinct Police Station, saying "THIS SPACE IS NOW PROPERTY OF THE SEATTLE PEOPLE". Food and drink is largely free of charge, and the people have planted a community garden in Cal Anderson Park. The people within the Zone are working together, sharing that which they have. No one person is trying to take advantage of any other. The profit motive is conspicuous by its absence. It is only the more astute journalists who are referring to this as the Seattle Commune.

Inside the Zone, workers have held long "town halls" to discuss their plans and hash out a strategy. As a result of this, they have put forward a list of demands, which include:

Abolish Seattle Police Department
Ban Use of Armed Force
Remove Officers From Schools
Eradicate Juvenile Jails and Prisons
Distribute Reparitions to Victims of Police Brutality

It should come as no great surprise to anyone that Trump "disapproves" of these shenanigans, to put it politely. As he phrased it, "Domestic Terrorists have taken over Seattle, run by Radical Left Democrats". He also ordered the city and state officials to "Take back your city NOW. If you don't do it, I will. This is not a game. These ugly Anarchists must be stopped IMMEDIATELY. MOVE FAST".

Trump is absolutely correct when he says that this is not a "game". Aside from that, his statements are full of slander and threats. American workers who are exercising their democratic right to protest are not Terrorists and Anarchists. That is a fact, just as it is a fact that his threat to "take back the city" should be taken seriously. He fully intends to send in the American military, to *invade the state of Washington* and "take back" the city of Seattle.

In response, the governor of Washington had a few harsh words of his own for Trump: "A man who is totally incapable of governing should stay out of Washington states' business." In addition, the mayor of Seattle issued her own statement: "The threat to invade Seattle, to divide and incite violence, in our city is not only unwelcome, it would be illegal".

These two statements, by the governor of the state of Washington, as well as the mayor of the city of Seattle, are absolutely correct. This in no way changes the fact that Trump has just announced his plans to invade a soverign state.

The current situation in America bears striking similarities to the situation of Russia, in early 1917, in the months immediately following the bourgeois revolution of February-March, in which the Czar was overthrown. The capitalists and landlords then assumed undisputed power, under a democratic republic.

At that time, Lenin was living in Switzerland, as he had been exiled years earlier. Still, he was tracking the Russian revolution as best he could, and offering advice in his letters, known as his Letters From Afar. As he put it, the capitalists are "prepared to stoop to any brutality, to any crime, to ruin and strangle any number of citizens in order to preserve the 'sacred right of property' for themselves *and their class*". (italics by Lenin)

Over the years, the capitalists, the bourgeoisie, have not "changed their stripes". The bourgeoisie of all countries are completely reactionary. We too are cursed with the capitalists, the billionaires, the class of people known as the bourgeoisie. Without doubt, these American capitalists see the occupation of those few city blocks in the city of Seattle as a threat to their "sacred right of property", as indeed it is. For that reason, they too are "prepared to stoop to any brutality, to any crime, to ruin and strangle any number of citizens". Hence the plan of Tump to send the American military into the city of Seattle, which is strictly against the law, in the interests of "law and order". Trump is not bluffing. He refers to himself as the "law and order president". By that he means that he lays down the law and gives the orders. To hell with the Constitution!

There are other similarities between Russia of 1917 and America of today. At that time, in Russia, the common people, both workers and peasants, had been schooled in the previous Russian revolution, the three years of 1905-1907. That revolution had failed to overthrow the Czar, but it had succeeded in educating the Russian people. That experience served them well in the February-March revolution of 1917, in which the Czar was finally overthrown, as well as the November 7 revolution of the same year, in which the capitalists were also overthrown.

In the months following the momentous occasion of the February- March revolution, there appeared in Russia an organization, that which Lenin referred to as a "workers government". The people taking part in those organizations referred to themselves as the "Soviet of Workers Deputies". This particular organization first took shape in the capital city of Saint Petersburg. Lenin also referred to this organization of workers as an "embryo of a workers government, the representative of the interests of the entire mass of the poor section of the population" (italics by Lenin) In a short time, this organization of workers spread across all of Russia. It also spread to the Soviet of Soldiers Deputies and to the Soviet of Poor Peasants Deputies.

This was exceptionally important, for as Lenin went on to explain, this Soviet of Workers Deputies was nothing less than a "transition from the first stage of the revolution to the second, and why the slogan, the 'task of the day', at this day must be: *Workers, you have performed miracles of proletarian heroism, the heroism of the people, in the civil war against tsarism. You must perform miracles of organization, organization of the proletariat and of the whole people, to prepare the way for your victory in the second stage of the revolution.*" (italics by Lenin)

Of necessity, this "victory in the second stage of the revolution" was a reference to the planned overthrow of the bourgeoisie and the establishment of a socialist republic. There is no alternate, as there are *no other social forces* in the political arena, *nor can there be*. In Russia, 1917, as in America, 2020, it is the capitalists, the bourgeoisie, against the workers, the proletariat. The bourgeoisie stand for capitalism and the workers stand for socialism. There is no middle ground.

It is not a coincidence that the leaders of the newly formed Russian bourgeois republic, those who were members of the

Kerensky regime, referred to the Soviet of Workers Deputies as "Anarchists". This was nothing less than slander, just as Trump is referring to peaceful protesters as Anarchists and Terrorists. Such tactics, that of slander, is characteristic of the bourgeoisie. It is merely a screen to conceal the interests of the capitalists, those who are concerned only with making a profit. In the process of pursuing their lust for that profit, they introduce anarchy and starvation into the country. It is only the working class, the proletariat, who can introduce law and order into the country, making sure that the basic needs of all are met. In the process, starvation, homelessness and imperialist war will be abolished.

Now, here in America, many of the members of the public, common people, are veterans of various protest movements. These include the Civil Rights Movement, the Anti War Movement and more recently the Occupy Movement. Those people are no doubt sharing their experiences with the younger members of the Zone. This Zone is the rough equivalent of the Soviet of Workers Deputies within Russia of 1917. I should mention that the word Soviet means Council. Just as the Soviet of Workers Deputies spread across the country of Russia, we can expect the Zone of Seattle to spread across the country of America.

The capitalists, the bourgeoisie, the class of people of whom Trump is a member, is also well aware of this. They too expect these self described Autonomous Zones to take shape in various cities and towns, and even to spread to the military, possibly in a different form, just as the Soviet of Soldiers Deputies made an appearance and spread across Russia. After all, the capitalists are not entirely stupid. They see the Zone as a threat to their authority, which is precisely what it is! For that reason, Trump is determined to "nip it in the bud".

The Capital Hill Autonomous Zone, CHAZ, is nothing less than a working class, proletarian area of occupation, within a vast sea of capitalism. The bourgeoisie view this as a "cancer" which could well spread throughout the whole "organism" if left unchecked. For that reason, they are determined to wipe it out. For the same reason, we are equally determined to offer it all support.

The fact is that we live in a class society, under capitalism. The capitalists are in charge, and we live under the dictatorship of the bourgeoisie. They rule! These parasites must be overthrown and capitalism must be replaced with socialism. The one and only way to do this is through revolution. After the bourgeoisie are overthrown, they must be crushed under the Dictatorship of the Proletariat. That is a fundamental tenet of Marxism.

Another fact is that there can be one and only one class in power, at any given time. Either the bourgeoisie is in charge, or the proletariat is in charge. The workers of Seattle have occupied a section of the city which they consider to be "Autonomous". For this they deserve a great deal of credit. It was a major accomplishment, a huge step forward on the road to revolution and scientific socialism. This is not to say that the Zone is Autonomous, because it is not.

It does mean that this is a *transitional* moment, a time of passing to the next stage of the revolution. It is the duty of Marxists to learn from the experience of previous revolutions, to understand precisely the *peculiarities* of this *transitional* moment, and from those peculiarities, to determine the tactics which must be followed.

With that in mind, it is safe to say that the revolutionary motion is becoming ever stronger. Each day, more people are marching and protesting. As I write this, yet another Black man has been killed by a White policeman, this time in the city of Atlanta. He is reported to have committed the "crime" of sleeping in his car. Ever more citizens are rising up in protest.

Further, the Chairman of the Joint Chiefs of Staff has issued an apology to the members of the public, for the role he played in the "photo op" of Trump in front of a church. Even the top military people are standing up to Trump! They are joining the ranks of the politicians, including the governors, mayors and members of the federal government, who are opposing Trump.

We can conclude by saying that the strength of the revolutionary motion is rising, growing ever stronger, while the capitalists are deeply divided. This in no way changes the fact that the American bourgeoisie and the American bourgeois intelligentsia are still very strong, deeply entrenched. They must be overthrown and then crushed under the Dictatorship of the Proletariat. The only solution is that the *proletariat must be organized!* The one and only way to achieve *durable victory* in the forthcoming revolution is to perform *miracles of proletarian organization!*

Even after the revolution, we will still need a revolutionary *government, a state.* That is what distinguishes us from the anarchists. The difference between revolutionary Marxists and the anarchists is that the Marxists are *for* utilizing revolutionary forms of the state, in the form of the Dictatorship of the Proletariat, after the revolution, while the anarchists are against this.

Organization is the slogan of the moment. This is *not* to say that workers should only join trade unions and mainstream political parties. They should also form Zones, or "Communes", if you prefer, modelled on the Seattle Autonomous Zone. Such Zones are certainly not legal, but should be set up all across the country, in all cities and towns. This should result in a fine combination of legal and illegal activity. These Zones must be regarded as organs of insurrection, of revolutionary rule, if only in embryonic form, because that is precisely what they are.

To suggest that working people should confine themselves to strictly legal activity is to work in the service of the social chauvinists and the centrists, those who are determined to maintain the rule of the bourgeoisie. Such legal activity is completely acceptable to the bourgeoisie, as it is not a threat to their rule. The creation of Zones or Communes is very much a threat to the rule of the bourgeoisie.

Now is the time to organize the proletariat. The people who have proven to be excellent organizers in the recent past are the American women and students. You have worked miracles of organization before, and you can do so again. As the proletarian revolution is very close, there is a crying need for your services. As you have the talent and skill, you also have a moral obligation to put those skills to good use. Now is no time to rest on your laurels. It is in the best interests of revolution, of scientific socialism, of the proletariat, that you once again organize. Only this time, do not limit yourself to Trump. Broaden your horizons. Go for the throat. Focus on destroying the bourgeoisie. Focus on the Dictatorship of the Proletariat. With that in mind, may I suggest organizing zones in all towns and cities, and not just small blocks. Occupy the whole town, the whole city. Occupy the whole state. Put the "Autonomous" in Autonomous Zones. Organize groups of states. Form separate socialist independent republics. Let the bourgeoisie know that the American founding fathers gave all Americans the right to "abolish any government which does not represent them", and that is just what you are doing. In short:

Organize the Proletariat!
Create More Autonomous Zones!

www.ingramcontent.com/pod-product-compliance
Lightning Source LLC
Chambersburg PA
CBHW032050020426
42335CB00011B/268